ROUTLEDGE LIBRARY EDITIONS: TRANSLATION

Volume 3

TRANSLATION AS SOCIAL ACTION

TRANSLATION AS SOCIAL ACTION
Russian and Bulgarian Perspectives

EDITED AND TRANSLATED
BY PALMA ZLATEVA
CHAPTER INTRODUCTIONS
BY ANDRÉ LEFEVERE

LONDON AND NEW YORK

First published in 1993 by Routledge

This edition first published in 2019
by Routledge
2 Park Square, Milton Park, Abingdon, Oxon OX14 4RN

and by Routledge
52 Vanderbilt Avenue, New York, NY 10017

Routledge is an imprint of the Taylor & Francis Group, an informa business

© 1993 Palma Zlateva

All rights reserved. No part of this book may be reprinted or reproduced or utilised in any form or by any electronic, mechanical, or other means, now known or hereafter invented, including photocopying and recording, or in any information storage or retrieval system, without permission in writing from the publishers.

Trademark notice: Product or corporate names may be trademarks or registered trademarks, and are used only for identification and explanation without intent to infringe.

British Library Cataloguing in Publication Data
A catalogue record for this book is available from the British Library

ISBN: 978-1-138-36785-2 (Set)
ISBN: 978-0-429-42953-8 (Set) (ebk)
ISBN: 978-1-138-36771-5 (Volume 3) (hbk)
ISBN: 978-1-138-36780-7 (Volume 3) (pbk)
ISBN: 978-0-429-42963-7 (Volume 3) (ebk)

Publisher's Note
The publisher has gone to great lengths to ensure the quality of this reprint but points out that some imperfections in the original copies may be apparent.

Disclaimer
The publisher has made every effort to trace copyright holders and would welcome correspondence from those they have been unable to trace.

Translation as Social Action

Russian and Bulgarian Perspectives

Edited and translated by Palma Zlateva
Chapter introductions by André Lefevere

London and New York

First published 1993
by Routledge
11 New Fetter Lane, London EC4P 4EE

Simultaneously published in the USA and Canada
by Routledge
29 West 35th Street, New York, NY 10001

© 1993 Palma Zlateva

Typeset in 10/12pt Baskerville by
ROM-Data Corp. Ltd, Falmouth, Cornwall
Printed and bound in Great Britain by
T J Press (Padstow) Ltd, Cornwall

All rights reserved. No part of this book may be reprinted or reproduced or utilized in any form or by any electronic, mechanical, or other means, now known or hereafter invented, including photocopying and recording, or in any information storage or retrieval system, without permission in writing from the publishers.

British Library Cataloguing in Publication Data
Zlateva, Palma
  Translation as Social Action. –
  (Translation Studies Series)
  I. Title II. Series
  418

Library of Congress Cataloging in Publication Data
  Translation as Social Action / Palma Zlateva [editor].
  p. cm. – (Translation studies)
  Includes bibliographical references and index.
  1. Translating and interpreting. 2. Translating and
  interpreting – Europe, Eastern – History. I. Zlateva, Palma,
  II. Series: Translation studies (London, England)
P306.2.T737 1993
418'.02 – dc20

92-28387
CIP

ISBN 0-415-07696-X pbk
ISBN 0-415-07695-1

Contents

	General editors' preface	vii
	Introduction	1
1	Categories for the study of translation *Anna Lilova*	5
2	Essential features and specific manifestations of historical distance in original texts and their translations *Iliana Vladova*	11
3	The theory and practice of translation *Jakob Retsker*	18
4	Interlanguage asymmetry and the prognostication of transformations in translation *Vladimir Gak*	32
5	The problem of the unit of translation *Leonid Barkhudarov*	39
6	Equivalence and adequacy *Alexander Shveitser*	47
7	A note on phrasemic calquing *Andrei Danchev*	57
8	Norms in translation *Vilen Komissarov*	63

9	Comprehension, style, translation, and their interaction *Margarita Brandes*	76
10	A psychological analysis of translation as a type of speech activity *Irina Zimnyaya*	87
11	A cognitive approach to translation equivalence *Bistra Alexieva*	101
12	Sense and its expression through language *Leonora Chernyakhovskaya*	110
13	Realia in translation *Sider Florin*	122
	Index	129

General editors' preface

The growth of translation studies as a separate discipline is a success story of the 1980s. The subject has developed in many parts of the world and is clearly destined to continue developing well into the twenty-first century. Translation studies brings together work in a wide variety of fields, including linguistics, literary study, history, anthropology, psychology, and economics. This series of books will reflect the breadth of work in translation studies and will enable readers to share in the exciting new developments that are taking place at the present time.

Translation is, of course, a rewriting of an original text. All rewritings, whatever their intention, reflect a certain ideology and a poetics and as such manipulate literature to function in a given society in a given way. Rewriting is manipulation, undertaken in the service of power, and in its positive aspect can help in the evolution of a literature and a society. Rewritings can introduce new concepts, new genres, new devices, and the history of translation is the history also of literary innovation, of the shaping power of one culture upon another. But rewriting can also repress innovation, distort and contain, and in an age of ever increasing manipulation of all kinds, the study of the manipulative processes of literature as exemplified by translation can help us toward a greater awareness of the world in which we live.

Since this series of books on translation studies is the first of its kind, it will be concerned with its own genealogy. It will publish texts from the past that illustrate its concerns in the present, and will publish texts of a more theoretical nature immediately addressing those concerns, along with case studies illustrating manipulation through rewriting in various literatures. It will be comparative in nature and will range through many literary traditions, both

Western and non-Western. Through the concepts of rewriting and manipulation, this series aims to tackle the problem of ideology, change and power in literature and society and so assert the central function of translation as a shaping force.

Susan Bassnett
André Lefevere

Introduction

Since the time of Czar Peter the Great, Russians have massively translated literary and other texts from other European nations. In fact, translation was one more "window" opened on the West, and many Russian writers and intellectuals considered translation an obvious part of their endeavor. As a result, translation and translators were, and are, highly respected, more so than in Western Europe or the Americas.

The same attitude toward translation persisted during the time of Soviet domination. In fact, the World Literature Series published under the direction of Maxim Gorky from 1918 to 1927 established the canon of "world literature" for the Soviet reader for decades to come.

Because the tradition of translation in Russia does not go back as far as it does in other European countries, and because it has always enjoyed greater respect, it has been able to develop in a less defensive manner. The whole debate on translatability, which paralyzed translation studies in the West for at least two decades after 1945, did not exert any comparable influence in Russia. The Russian tradition, and other traditions such as the Bulgarian, with which it has been linked historically, does not therefore have a similar record of mental acrobatics designed to reconcile two utterly irreconcilable positions, namely (i) that translation is impossible and (ii) that hundreds of thousands of translations have been made, are made, and will continue to be made and used for as long as people speak different languages and are members of different cultures. Since Russian and Bulgarian students of translation decided to study translations that were made, rather than try to prove why translations could not be made, they developed a more systematic and consistent apparatus for the analysis of existing translations than their colleagues in the West have done until now. The critical vocabulary in Russian and Bulgarian studies of translation is stable, unlike that used in corresponding Western studies, where many a beginning translation scholar feels strangely compelled to reinvent the wheel time and again, either by ignoring the work of his or her colleagues or by unnecessarily terrorizing them by subjecting them to a whole lexicon of new terms designating well-known phenomena and coined for no particular reason other than the one just mentioned. The tradition represented by the essays collected in this book is also very conscious of its own historical dimension, and therefore tackles problems connected with the history of translation with greater frequency and at greater length than has been done until recently in the West.

But perhaps the most salient difference between the tradition represented here and its Western counterpart is that the former has for some time considered translation as, in Anna Lilova's words, "a social, cultural, and creative activity" – in other words, a form of meaningful action, not the meaningless drudgery to be performed by underpaid intellectuals in the West, the strange "non-labor" performed by shadowy "transparent" translators whose names, until recently, were only rarely printed together with their work since translators were, after all, deemed to be engaged in vitally necessary but utterly impossible activities. Because it views translation as a meaningful act, the tradition represented here goes far beyond the domain of language. While obviously acknowledging the central part played by language in translation, it does not try to separate language from the social, historical, and cultural context in which it operates. This is not to say that it is incapable of dealing with language on any level of abstraction. On the contrary. But where it deals with language on that level it does so to make matters clearer, not to obliterate the links between language and other fields. In other words, it makes a virtue of abstraction, not a goal.

The tradition represented here also tries to strike a viable balance between "theory" and "practice." It does not presume to formulate universally valid rules for translation, but neither is it willing to declare that all it describes and analyzes is of no use to practicing translators who feel increasingly "betrayed" by the more theoretical and abstract study of translation in Western Europe and the Americas. However, just as linguists compiling descriptive grammars of languages do, in effect, also codify current usage which is accepted as some kind of "norm," translation scholars also codify translational norms, current and/or past. The distinction between codifying norms and imposing them is vital here: translation scholars codify practice and offer it for possible guidance, but the final decision always remains with the translator, who is, after all, a human being capable of making decisions, not a machine that is fed originals, blindly performs some abstract rule-governed operations, and "outputs" a translation.

Significantly, essays collected in this volume tend to become more abstract when they deal with problems unlikely to yield anything that may prove of immediate practical use for translators in the field. Just as significantly these problems are very rarely dealt with outside the tradition represented here. The psychological aspect of translation has until recently been widely neglected in Western Europe and the Americas, precisely because translation has always been considered a derived, secondary activity, of very limited import and expected only to yield immediate and, preferably, reliable results. Yet the tradition represented here also has its less positive characteristics. Perhaps the most obvious is the heavy, almost exclusive reliance on a positivistic ideal of science that tends to be viewed as out of date in the West. The question arises as to what extent scholars working inside the tradition represented here not only were cut off from recent developments in the philosophy of science, but also were constrained to work under the shadow of more or less dogmatic Marxism–Leninism as institutionalized in the former Soviet Union.

In this respect it is easy to see how the attempt to analyze and describe translations in a more rigorous fashion originates in the very justified desire to rise beyond the anecdotal that tended to mar and still mars so much discourse on translation. It is less easy to see, though, whether the method used to attain this kind of rigor actually manages to achieve its goal without resulting in pointless overkill.

There cannot be the shadow of a doubt that the conceptual frameworks that readers are confronted with here are well constructed, on the basis of empirical observation in most, and along lines drawn with strict logical rigor in all cases. Yet doubt tends to arise occasionally as to their immediate, or even long-term, relevance. One cannot help wondering, for instance, why Barchudarov goes to such length describing the phonemic and morphemic levels of units of translation, only to admit in the same breath that they hardly ever occur.

There is also a certain rhetoric inside the Russian and Bulgarian tradition that tends to smack of the ponderous at times. This is all the more regrettable since this kind of rhetoric would not infrequently manage to overshadow valuable insights – if one let it. The editor has therefore exercised her stylistic privileges to the full, and occasionally somewhat beyond, to make sure this would not be allowed to happen. She has, in other words, used her creativity to ensure communication at the expense of narrowly defined equivalence. She has done so because she believes that the texts contained in this book are of great potential value for students of translation who have not had access to them in the past. They show a different tradition, trying to grapple in ways that are different and yet recognizable with what are likely to be the most important topics in translation studies for quite a while to come: the shaping and breaking of cultural, ethnic, and historical images that function as the only reality that a culture is able to ascribe to other cultures it does not know but has to live with.

Chapter 1
Categories for the study of translation

Anna Lilova

The categories proposed in the essay that follows may strike the reader as somewhat grandiose, or even chimeric, but this reaction itself is symptomatic of a fundamental problem in the study of translation in the West and, to a lesser extent, also still in the East.

Lilova points out, and rightly so, that translation is the product of history, not science. In other words, translation arose in response to specific social, historical, and cultural demands. Translations have been produced for centuries in Europe, but because the activity of translating as such has never been able to claim a relatively high social status, the study of translation has rarely been institutionalized in the educational programs of the very countries that produced translations over the centuries.

Because the production of translations has never been held in high esteem in the West, the study of both the process and the product has been relegated to the margins of educational institutions. There are many departments of language, linguistics, and literature in the universities of Eastern and Western Europe and the Americas, but very few departments of translation studies.

This situation has not changed much since translation studies as a discipline began to come into its own about ten to fifteen years ago. Translation studies is therefore still a discipline without an institutional base. This, more than anything else, explains the categories proposed here and the grandiose schemes in which they are embedded in similar essays written by translation scholars in East and West: they are born of frustration to no small extent. They are, if you will, radically and unrepentingly nominalist: by building up a viable discipline in words, they hope to somehow conjure up the institutional support for those words.

They have never been very successful in doing so, and this very fact opens up another debate: is it necessary to establish an independent "megadiscipline" of translation studies, complete with all the trappings of the trade, or is it more realistic to view translation studies as a concept that can be studied within existing disciplines and their institutional bases? The debate is by no means over.

A. L.

Translation is a multilevel and multilateral phenomenon, each aspect of which is just as important as any other. Any reduction of the complexity, any subordination of one aspect to another, would widen the gap between our knowledge of translation and the actual phenomenon of translation itself. The generic notion of "translation" covers such drastically distinct forms of translation as oral translation (interpretation), written translation, machine translation, literary translation, scientific, technical, and socio-political translation. Translation has linguistic, literary, aesthetic, psychological, and other characteristic features. They should all be taken into consideration in any study of translation.

The system of different types of translation has evolved historically in the process of the social and spiritual development both of mankind as a whole and of every separate country and people in particular. In other words, the system of translation as an entity, made up of different forms, types, and genres, is the product of history, not the product of science, and it develops in the context of history which makes it richer and more perfect. Therefore, the historical category should play a basic part in the study of the system and the clarification of its typological problems. The system of the various forms of translation is an *objective historical entity, governed by laws*, because it is the very flow of human history that brought the forms of translation, both oral and written, to life.

The system of the various forms of translation is a *dynamic* one. When sound was added to the silent movie, film translation was born with its specific artistic and cinematographic demands, such as the synchronization of dialogue and its coordination with the action that takes place on the screen. Film translation was followed by translation for television with its own specific demands tailored to the small screen.

In my opinion, the *functional* category should also play a basic part in any attempt to study translation. Undoubtedly the system of translation has been shaped in history as a whole and in the development of separate nations according to the social needs, artistic (in all their variants), scientific, technical, political, and others depending on the social functions of translation. The process of differentiation of the types of translation is the result of continuous and stable social needs. Certain types or genres of translation may lose their significance or change their function as the social or individual need for them dies out. That is why any approach to the study of translation should be based on the historical and social concept of culture as a whole. We should relate the process of appearance, development, and disappearance, of differentiation and unification of the various forms, types, and genres of translation to functional needs and national prerequisites.

The next category, which I shall conventionally call the *genetic* one, addresses the genetic connection between the typology of translation and the typology of original literature. To ignore this obvious connection would be both baseless and wrong. It is only too clear that the various types of translation, though relatively autonomous, are not formed independently and in isolation from the types and genres of the originals they attempt to translate.

The genesis and development of the system of different kinds of translations and its typology is a function of the mutual cultural ties among peoples. The interaction between the system of various kinds of original texts and that of translations as an integral part of the mutual relations between two cultures is not mechanical in nature. It is a process that takes place either directly, as a result of the interaction between two given cultures, or indirectly, with a third culture acting as a mediator between two other cultures. This process is characterized by numerous tendencies and phenomena, which accounts for the complexity and even delicacy of the genetic ties between translation typology and the typology of the original literature.

Another category, just as important, in my opinion, for the study of translation, is that of *structure and content*. To grasp the specific nature of the forms, types, and genres of translation we should first of all analyze the translated text, its structure and its content, and ask ourselves the following three questions: (i) What does this text express or contain? (ii) Who is it meant for? (iii) For what purpose is it translated?

In spite of all the positive features of structural analysis I believe that, no matter what the structure of the translated text is, it does not exist by itself as an abstract, static value. Rather it is connected both to the original, which belongs to a given historical and social context, and to its own new social, cultural, and linguistic reality.

A *psychological* category is also needed in the study of translation. This covers translation as a whole, both in the manner of its production and in the manner of its reception, the specific work the translator does in various forms, types, and genres of translation, and the degree of creativity characteristic of each of them.

The *degree of creativity* in different genres and forms of translation plays a very important part in the study of translation. The laws defining translation as a specific creative act are objective in character. Let us take translation on the level of language, for instance, even though the levels of talent, erudition, and general culture are also extremely significant. The whole transition from the primary verbal text of the original to the newly created secondary text of the translation is an activity connected with language. Unlike a literary text, in which the expressive potential of the form – the language – strongly resists the translator's efforts, a scientific text is not as sensitive to form. The Bulgarian scholar A. Lyudskanov was therefore right to remark on the existence of regulated and non-regulated choices in the translation process. The different degrees of resistance of the verbal material are responsible for the typological and generic discrimination between literary and non-literary translation (Lyudskanov 1967).

Shveitser also pointed out that "the creative and the non-creative beginning is present in every type of translation; they are closely interwoven, even though their distribution changes according to the genre of translation" (1973: 18).

Creative moments exist in all forms of translation, but if we take the specific character of the literary text into account we cannot deny that the level of creativity in literary translation is higher indeed. Creativity in translation should, in my opinion, be understood as (i) creativity on the level of language (which can therefore be present in all types of translation) and (ii) creativity on the level of artistic and imaginative thinking and recreation.

The specificity of literary translation would therefore appear to lie beyond the limit of linguistic creativity which is present in all forms, types, and genres of translation. This implies that we also leave the sphere behind in which all variations of translation begin: the sphere of language, since language cannot fully account for the process of translation and its results. The difference between the language of literature and that of science is not just a difference of form but also a difference of content. This difference in turn demands different ways of shaping the original, and of reshaping it in translation.

This brings us to the basic and most important category in the study of translation: the *linguistic* category which includes the specific nature of languages, the peculiarities of linguistic means of expression, of lexical and phraseological elements, of grammatical forms and syntactic constructions, and of the different styles connected with different types of genres of translation.

Why do I select the linguistic category as one of the major categories underlying any study of translation? Because of the basic and indisputable fact that language is the building material, the tangible entity present in both original and translation. Consequently, this principle reflects the real linguistic characteristics and peculiarities of literary, scientific, and socio-political translation which in their turn represent the basic qualities and distinguishing features of the various types of translation.

This does not mean, however, that the linguistic category should be the only category on which distinctions between the different types and genres of translations are to be based. In fact, this is precisely the weakness of many current typologies, in particular those elaborated by Katharina Reiss and Hans J. Vermeer. Exclusive reliance on this category is, in my opinion, both methodologically and factually wrong, simply because no single category, no matter how important, can exhaust the complex nature and systematicity of translation as a specific social, cultural, and creative activity.

The basic categories enumerated above should be supplemented by a number of additional features that play their part in the differentiation of forms, types, and genres of translation. Such features are the physical peculiarities of the language of the written translation, which has a fixed dimension and exists in time, as well as the various ways in which receivers (readers or listeners) perceive the translated text through the intermediary of various senses, as in the case of visual, audio-visual, or auditory translation.

WORKS CITED

Lyudskanov, A. (1967) *Prevezhdat chovekat i mashinata* [*Man and Machine Translate*], Sofia: Nauka i izkustvo.

Reiss, K. (1976) *Texttyp und Übersetzungsmethode*, [*Texttype and Translation Method*], Kronberg: Taurus.

Reiss, K. and Vermeer, H. J. (1984) *Grundlegung einer allgemeinen Translationstheorie* [*The Foundation of a General Theory of Translation*], Tübingen: Niemeyer.

Shveitser, A. (1973) *Perevod i lingvistika* [*Translation and Linguistics*], Moscow: Voenizdat.

Chapter 2

Essential features and specific manifestations of historical distance in original texts and their translations

Iliana Vladova

Time is an important factor in translation. It makes re-translations of already translated texts necessary, but it also makes internal translations necessary, that is, translations within the same language, from one historical period (say, the medieval period) to another (say, the modern period). But time can also be manipulated by authors of original texts. They may go back to an older stage of the language and weave it into their text for all kinds of reasons. Similarly, they may also refer to things or concepts no longer current in their own time.

The translation of these archaizing elements in the original poses a problem. If they are simply leveled in the translation, that is, if they are translated into the same stage of the target language as the rest of the text, they obviously will no longer achieve any effect at all. Yet, what stage of the target language could be said to be "equivalent" to the stage of the source language the original author weaves into the original text? Or what things and concepts contemporary in the translator's world can be said to be "equivalent" to the things and objects no longer contemporary in the writer's world when he or she wrote the original?

These features of translation make "theorists" uneasy, especially theorists who think of translators as "transparent rule-following mechanical entities," because they highlight aspects of the original text that will always point to the "translatedness" of the translation. No matter what solution the translator provides, it will inevitably draw the reader's attention to the fact that he or she is reading a translation that is the result of the process of the labor of one or more individuals, and this will undermine, or even destroy altogether, the cherished illusion of the "transparent" translation.

And once translation is no longer perceived as routinely transparent, it runs the risk of being thematized as problematic beyond the charmed circle of translation scholars.

Russian and Bulgarian scholars of translation have probably been confronted with this problem more often than their colleagues in the West because of the avowed cultural policy of the Soviet state that called for the classics of the non-Russian republics to be translated into Russian. Translators were forced to think about the matter in more detail and to come up with their own solutions.

A. L.

The term "historical distance" is not unambiguous. Translation theorists tend to invest it with different meanings, expanding or contracting its radius of application as they do so. They also devise different approaches to the solution of the problem of distance in time manifested in works of fiction.

The most generally held normative assumption wants a translator to reveal and stress the historical setting of the original as much as possible (Antokol'skij *et al.* 1955: *passim*). This assumption can be considered axiomatic for every adequate literary translation, but the features that constitute the historical specificity of the original differ in nature.

In his long article "Distance in time and translation" devoted to Russian translations of Benjamin Constant's *Adolphe*, Jakobsen's *Frau Maria Grube*, and Rabelais' *Gargantua and Pantagruel*, Andres does not distinguish between different types of historical distance. Rather, he reduces them all to a common denominator and suggests that the problem of historical distance can simply be solved by projecting the translation on the stylistic peculiarities of the receiving literature (Andres 1964: 129).

L'vov (1967) takes a more differentiated approach to the study of historical distance. His analysis, situated within the framework of linguistics, distinguishes between three types of historical distance in the language of the original. One type manifests itself in the natural aging of the language of the original as a result of the application of the objective laws of its development. A second type manifests itself in the form of purposeful archaization of the language of the original by the author himself, who reveals past times and events in his work. The third type is a combination of the other two.

L'vov's distinction is productive and scientifically well-founded since it is based on objective criteria, such as the natural development of a language. Yet historical distance can also manifest itself in other components of a work of fiction. Moreover, L'vov is mostly concerned with the theoretical investigation of the problem and he does not offer any practical suggestions for dialectically neutralizing historical distance in translation. Rather, he limits himself to the statement that the problem of preserving historical perspective does not admit simple and universal solutions.

Kardosh (1967) offers more concrete opinions in his study which deals with both the levels and the forms of archaization permissible in translation. Kardosh holds that archaization is permissible only when the author of the original has resorted to such linguistic means of expression as were no longer used by his or her contemporaries. The problem of the translation of a work of fiction written in a language that is neutral for its original reader but outdated for the contemporary consumer of the original artifact calls for an entirely different solution.

In translating such works we should use our contemporary language to help the reader of the translation to experience a reception of the text that approximates the reception of the original as closely as possible. The translator should evoke in the reader's mind the atmosphere of the historical setting of the original and stress its outdatedness by means of the use of contemporary language.

The studies mentioned above deal with both the different artistic and aesthetic concepts characterizing a given period in time and the proper balance to be struck between the contemporary and archaic elements of a language. The solution of the problem of historical distance is reduced to either the stylistic parameters of the receiving literature or the archaisms available in the translator's language. The studies mentioned therefore show themselves to be either literary or linguistic in nature.

Representatives of the linguistic approach restrict the historical to linguistic signs only. They focus on revealing the linguistic processes, the material bearers of information contained in a given work of historical fiction. Historical distance is thought to have been carried across in an acceptable manner if the linguistic units that carry the historical flavor of the original are adequately matched with linguistic units in the translation.

Representatives of the literary approach concentrate on the stylistic peculiarities of the historical text and restrict, or even ignore, the meaning of language by projecting them onto the receiving literature. They reduce the adequacy of a translation to a recreation of the original in its aesthetic manifestation irrespective of the means by which that has been achieved.

Without being pedantic, we can state in a most general way that the linguistic approach solves the problem of the form, the so-called bearer of information. It fails, however, to penetrate deeply into the content conveyed by this information and to grasp its historical character as contained in the original and, afterwards, also in the translation. The literary approach, on the other hand, considers historical distance from the vantage point of the laws and regularities of the literary process, the artistic realization of the content of the original.

Yet when analyzed separately to whatever possible degree, neither the form nor the content aspect of a work of fiction can serve as a basis for a systematic scientific approach to the problem, since form and content form a unity in their dialectic interrelationship. "The infringement of the principle of unity in favor of one or the other of these two basic components not only results in theoretical inconsistencies, but also causes practical harm to the translation itself" (Gachechiladze 1970: 123).

Neither the linguistic nor the literary approach can claim priority on the basis of the well-foundedness of its analysis of, and the value of its solutions to, the problem of historical distance in translation. If we assume that translation is an artistic, functional, and stylistic expression of the content and ideas of the original, the problem of historical distance should be tackled both from the linguistic and the literary angle.

Literary translation is a creative process in which translators not only reveal the content of the original by means of suitable linguistic expression; they also repeat the original creative process experienced by the author of the prototext in that translators give that prototext a new lease of life in a new social, historical, and national environment. If we analyze the informational aspect of translation we can study it as a process in action, a functioning act of communication governed by strict laws and regularities.

This act of communication involves the author, the translator, and the reader. All three have their own concept of the information that is not just embodied in the original message, but inextricably bound to it. In the process of communication they enter into different relationships with regard to the categories of space and time. If we are able to formulate those relationships we may also be able to solve the problem at hand.

There is a distance in time between the author's concrete historical world that has shaped his or her creative individual vision and served as a source for the refraction that results in the original, and the world in which the translator lives, works, and translates. This type of historical distance determines all the components of a work of fiction. It is revealed in its thematic nucleus, in its system of images, and in its form. Or, in Anna Lilova's words: "Language is directed toward the text, since it derives its form from that text, but it is also directed toward everything that is outside the text since that reveals the connection between the text and the outside world" (1981: 147). It is here that a natural archaization sets in, followed by objective laws of development.

Translators must bring the ideas, the images, and the peculiarities of the stylistic system that correspond to given aesthetic principles and criteria of value across to the reader's consciousness. They must do so in such a way as to bring the original closer to their contemporaries by overcoming historical distance. Yet they must also show, by means of adequate linguistic devices, that the original is a refraction of a concrete historical stage in the development of a given nation, its social and political system, its economic structure, its spiritual values, and its language. In other words, translators must reflect the dialectics of historical development, ideas, language, and artistic devices.

Nor is this the only type of historical distance in translation. Historical distance also obtains between the concrete historical reality that served as the source of refraction for authors, and the concrete historical reality in which they were brought up and which shaped their individual creative consciousness. In this case authors make up their own concept for transforming this reality removed in time, and for overcoming the distance between the text and the reader. They will use those stylistic and linguistic devices that will have to identify the events that serve as the source of their artistic refraction. Translators are called upon to reveal their author's concept by means of stylistic and linguistic devices.

In the case of this second type of historical distance the language of the translation will be shaped not only by the contemporary state of the national language of the receiving culture, but also by elements that belong to its passive resources. In this case translators should bear the time coordinates of those passive resources in mind since it would not be advisable to use any that do not belong in the historical period refracted in the original.

There is a third possibility: the events narrated in the original take place in one concrete period of time, the author's world is part of another period, and translators live in yet another period. This type of historical distance is manifested in the original in a very peculiar way. Not only does it reflect the author's concept of history (as did the second type); it also reflects the changes that have taken place in the language as the result of the objective laws of history. Translators find themselves still further removed from the original because of this historical retrospective. In translating such a text they will have to form their own concept of it, based on an amalgam of the author's historical concept, the objective concept of the time, and the concept of their contemporary reader, the intended reader of the translation.

Finally, we can distinguish yet another, fourth type of historical distance. It constitutes the logical answer to the questions: 'Why do translations grow old? Why do new historical epochs call for new translations?' There is a peculiar distance between two concrete historical periods that each make their own demands on translation, and those demands originate in the aesthetic needs of their respective periods in time, since human society carries out a revaluation of its values in every stage of its development. Along with all this, translators' criteria and principles also evolve. Language naturally plays a major part in the process of this evolution since it, too, is influenced by the time factor and subject to different changes.

The formulation of these four types of historical distance rests on definite relationships that characterize the author as the subject of the refraction of reality in the original, the translator as the subject of the secondary refraction of this reality which, having passed through the author's creative imagination, has already become an artistic reality, and the reader as the addressee of the aesthetic information carried by the original.

The first type of historical distance is based on the relationship "subject of the refraction"–"subject of the secondary refraction." The second type is based on the relationship "subject of the refraction"–"object of the refraction." The third type manifests itself in the triple chain "object of the refraction"–"subject of the refraction"–"subject of the secondary refraction" in the course of which first one participant in the communicative act comes to the fore, and then the other. The fourth type focuses attention on readers as consumers of the original artifact, although they have their place in the other three types as well. Like authors and translators, readers are also connected to a concrete historical medium and concrete conditions that have shaped their consciousness, their aesthetic tastes and reactions, and therefore also their ability to grasp a certain original produced within definite temporal parameters.

WORKS CITED

Andres, A. (1964) "Distancia vremeni i perevod" [Distance in time and translation], *Masterstvo perevoda* [*The Mastery of Translation*], Moscow: Sovetskij pisatel', 118–31.

Antokol'skij, P., Auzov, M., and Ril'skij, M. (1955) "Hudozhestvennye perevody literatury narodov SSSR" [The literary translations of the works of fiction of the peoples of the USSR], *Voprosy hudozhestvennogo perevoda* [*Problems of Literary Translation*], Moscow: Sovetskij pisatel'.

Gachechiladze, G. R. (1970) *Vvedenie v teoriju hudozhestvennogo perevoda* [*An Introduction to the Theory of Literary Translation*], Tbilisi: Tbilisi University.

Kardosh, L. (1967) "Aktual'nye problemy teorii hudozhestvennogo perevoda" [Topical problems in the theory of literary translation], *Sovet po hudozhestvennomu perevodu* [*Board on Literary Translation*], vol. 1, Moscow: Sojuz pisatelej SSSR, 165–70.

Lilova, A. (1981) *Uvod v obshtata teorija na prevoda* [*An Introduction to the General Theory of Translation*], Sofia: Narodna kultura.

L'vov, S. (1967) "Aktual'nye problemy teorii hudozhestvennogo perevoda" [Topical problems in the study of literary translation], *Sovet po hudozhestvennomu perevodu* [*Board on Literary Translation*], vol. 2, Moscow: Sojuz pisatelej SSSR, 245–53.

Chapter 3

The theory and practice of translation

Jakob Retsker

Some Russian scholars of translation have revalorized the term "variant" in their work. They suggest that translators substitute one "unit" (however defined) in one language for one "equivalent" (however defined) unit in another language in the least numerous, and often least interesting, cases. Most of the translators' time and effort is invested, on the contrary, in the creation of "variants." These variants represent the translators' personal choices – made, to be sure, on the basis of patterns that have been codified, taught, internalized, but the translators' own nevertheless.

These variants depend on a number of parameters, the most important of which may well be the communicative situation in which translators find themselves. This communicative situation is obviously not determined by translators alone, even though they probably work with some kind of "ideal" audience in mind. On the contrary, any kind of communicative situation presupposes interaction between producer and receiver. It would be a mistake to think, though, that this interaction is always freely entered into and freely carried out. Rather it should be remembered that any communicative situation is always embedded in a certain culture at a certain moment in history, and that any interaction in it is therefore likely to take place under some kinds of constraints.

The constraints that circumscribe a given communicative situation are likely to be recognized as very important factors, both in the process of translation and in the process of the reception of the finished product. Translators can go with the constraints or they can use translations to go against these constraints and to communicate what original texts may not be able to do at certain historical moments. Translators do not choose the communicative situations they work in, but they always retain the choice between reproducing their texts or refunctioning them.

A. L.

BASIC ASSUMPTIONS

It is the translator's task to render the content of the original in another language, precisely and exhaustively, while preserving its stylistic and expressive peculiarities. A translation's "exhaustive" character refers to the unity of form and content created on a new linguistic basis. If the criterion for a translation's exactness is indeed the identity of the information communicated in two different languages, then only a translation which renders that information by means of equivalent devices can be considered exact. In other words, unlike a retelling, a translation must render not only the *it*, whatever is expressed in the original, but also the *how*, the way in which it has been expressed. This requirement holds not only for the translation of a text as a whole, but also for the translation of its component parts.

We shall now leave aside the problem of the relationship between part and whole in the process of translation, since that problem requires special analysis, and concentrate on the notion of "equivalent devices."

Comparative linguistics is of great importance for the creation of a linguistic theory of translation. As a rule, comparative linguistics deals with just one part of language, be it grammar, vocabulary, or style. Data furnished by comparative linguists may therefore be used as the basis for a private theory of translation, that is, for a theory of translation formulated for a specific pair of languages. We should bear in mind, however, that the complex nature of translation calls for a complex comparative approach.

What matters to the translator is not the comparison of separate grammatical forms or syntactic constructions, but rather the comparison of whole structural-semantic nuclei that constitute one notional whole. The naked grammatical structure, stripped of its lexical content, is as meaningless for the translator as the metal frame of a house is for that house's future inhabitant. The categories of general translation theory are constructed on a double basis: both on the basis of data taken from private theories of translation and on the logico-semantic basis shared by a number of languages at a similar level of development. The task of a theory of fixed correspondence is to establish fixed parameters within which a choice of translational variants can be made. Without supplying prescriptions, a theory of regular correspondence establishes the main regular features of the process of translation, based on functional correspondence. When translating from one language into another we have to take into account the part played by identical factors of a logico-semantic nature in the rendering of identical factors of meaning. An initial reading and analysis of the original text enables us to establish in advance the nature of its contents, its concepts, and the stylistic peculiarities of its linguistic material. Having established these, we may then proceed to establish criteria for the choice of linguistic devices in the process of translation. In the course of an analysis of the original as described above, we are able to establish "units of translation" (separate words, expressions, or parts of sentences), for which permanent, stable correspondences exist in the target language. These correspondences are underwritten by established tradition. Such equivalent correspondences are very limited in number in individual texts. They are far smaller in number than other "units of translation" that can be rendered into another language only if the translator looks for correspondences in the rich resources of a language and proceeds to make a choice that is by no means arbitrary. This choice is of course not restricted to data fixed in a dictionary, since no dictionary can foresee all varieties of contextual meaning expressed in the actual flow of speech, not to mention the various possible combinations of words. For this reason a theory of translation can only establish functional correspondences that take into account that the rendering of given semantic categories is dependent on the action of different factors. This principle is also operational in establishing contextual meaning and in the realization of different lexical transformations. Contextual meaning is often established by means of extrapolation on the basis of possible meanings supplied by the dictionary, while lexical transformations operate according to the logico-semantic principle, but without neglecting factors of a stylistic and expressive nature.

Three categories of correspondence are therefore established in the process of translation: (i) the equivalent, established as the result of either identity of denotation or traditional interlanguage contact; (ii) the variant, or contextual correspondence; (iii) all types of translational transformations. A fundamental distinction exists between the first category and the other two: equivalents operate on the level of "langue," the other two categories on that of "parole." When segments of the flow of speech are processed to fit the norms of the receiving language during the process of translation, equivalents can be seen to stand out because of their relative regularity and also because they display a relative independence of their surroundings. Where traditional equivalent correspondences exist between two languages the translator has virtually no choice. Any refusal to use such an equivalent is a deviation that must be very well motivated by peculiarities of context or overall setting.

What are the criteria for the correct choice of devices designed to ensure the production of adequate translations? Since the criterion for adequacy can only be correspondence to the segment of reality depicted in the original, equivalence of devices is defined not by identity but by maximum approximation to the result achieved by the impact of the original. Any analysis of any highly professional achievements in translation will show that the basis for establishing equivalence of linguistic devices can only be functional, not formal, in nature. The complex process of translation encompasses too many factors that prevent the establishing of formal correspondences on the level of parole. One and the same linguistic form can perform different functions depending on a combination of different linguistic and non-linguistic factors. No doubt translators will have to resort to logic, psychology, and a knowledge of literature if they want to reflect the thoughts, emotions, and perceptions contained in the original adequately, but the text is and remains the only basis for their work, just as functional correspondence remains the basis for any linguistic approach to the text.

Yet the number and quality of factors creating the basis of this functional correspondence vary with different types of translated texts. What remains constant is the logico-semantic basis determining the processes of analysis and synthesis underlying all methods of translation, as will be shown later. Even the "penetration into reality," that is, the foundation of so-called denotative theories of translation, cannot serve as a criterion for adequacy in translation. It sometimes happens that translators are better and more deeply acquainted with a segment of reality depicted in an original than the author of that original himself. But are translators therefore justified in recreating this reality in a way that *differs* from that in which it is depicted in the original? Such an approach would vitiate the very essence of translation and substitute the translator's own vision of reality for the author's.

The distinction between linguistic and non-linguistic factors is accepted in thinking on translation. Nonetheless, it remains somewhat oversimplified, since much of what resorts under the second category is suggested both by the translated text and by the experience of the qualified translator. Even a given translator's degree of competence in a given field referred to in the original must be counted among the factors defining the functional basis for regular correspondence.

EQUIVALENT CORRESPONDENCES

The notion of "equivalent" in thinking about translation is twofold. "Equivalent" often means every correspondence to a word or combination of words in the original in a given concrete context or, in other words, every properly established correspondence to a macrounit of translation. Such a non-constructive understanding of equivalence, however, nullifies any significant difference between categories of dictionary equivalents. Rather, "equivalent" should be taken to mean a constant, regular, context-free correspondence. Equivalents are something like catalysts in the process of translation. It is hard to overestimate the part they play, particularly in the process of interpretation. These very units of translation, which exhibit regular correspondences in the native tongue, come to translator's minds and help them understand the meaning of the surrounding context, or of the whole utterance, even when either, or both, contain some unfamiliar words.

The data provided by bilingual dictionaries should obviously not be taken as the final truth in these matters, even though they represent a fairly adequate picture of the categories of words and expressions in one language that have just one equivalent correspondence in another. Geographical names come to mind, as do names of persons, and terms used in various fields of knowledge, but they are not the only ones. Page 400 of the *Big English–Russian Dictionary* edited by I. Gal'perin provides us with the following indubitable equivalents: doctrinarianism/doktrinerstvo, dodder/povilike, dodman/ulitka, dog-bee/truten', dog-bolt/otkidnyi bolt, dog-collar/osheinik. It would seem that combinations of words and compound words have equivalents more often than single words do. The overwhelming majority of English words have more than one meaning. Yet words with a transparent inner form often acquire one fixed meaning in the language, and one single correspondence, as illustrated by the list given above, in which the last three words are built on the image of "dog."

Equivalents can be full or partial, absolute or relative. All the examples quoted above are full equivalents, since they express the full meaning of the word, not just one of its meanings. "Dirt cheap" and "deshevle parenoi repy," on the other hand, are partial equivalents, because they have different stylistic and expressive colorings. "Shadow" has a partial equivalent in the basic meaning of "ten'," since the English word has the additional meanings of "polumrak" and "prizrak." Yet the combination "the shadow of the dog" undoubtedly has an absolute equivalent in its only possible correspondence: "sumerki bogov." The tradition of interlanguage correspondence is so stubborn that no other translation would be accepted.

Let us follow the process by which equivalences are established by taking the translation of neologisms as an example. When a new word appears in English, translators usually try to find the best and, if possible, only correspondence for it. This is particularly important in the field of terminology. "Supermarket," for instance, was initially translated as "sverhrynok," but the translation turned out to be inadequate because of its ambiguity. "Magazin bez prodavcov" also failed to find general acceptance and was consequently superseded by the now current equivalent "magazin samoobsluzhivaniya."

Strict accuracy in translation sometimes requires translators to go against the principle of language economy, as when "brinkmanship" is translated into "balansirovanie na grani voiny" and "a policy of brinkmanship" as "politika balansirovanie na grani voiny." The political neologism "sellout" also calls for a detailed translation: "predatel'stvo nacional'nyh interesov." On the other hand, it is sometimes possible to pick up short Russian equivalents for combinations of English words, as in "operativnost'" for "administrative efficiency," "kollegial'nost'" for "joint thinking," "disciplinirovannost'" for "spirit of discipline," and "perlyustraciya" for "mail cover check."

Catford's proposal to use "transfer" instead of "translation" should be explained by his refusal to consider equivalence as a possible way of rendering the meanings of source language words by making use of target language words. His reference to Peirce's opinion further spreads this skeptical attitude to the domain of whole utterances. But the very example Catford quotes (1965: 35) in support of this view shows plainly that the view itself is mistaken. "I have arrived" is not equal to "Ya prishel," since neither the grammatical nor the lexical element of the sentences overlaps. The lack of an equivalent, that is, of a constant equivalent correspondence, does not in the least prevent adequate rendering of the content by means of a different method, namely the use of variant correspondences, such as "Ya prishel," "Ya priehal," "Ya priletel," and even "Ya pribyl" in certain situations.

The existence of nine personal pronouns in some Indonesian languages, as opposed to seven in English, the absence of an English word for the Finnish "sauna," or the absence in English of the Russian connotation of the word "sputnik," that is, the lack of correspondence between separate lexical units that Catford refers to, by no means excludes the possibility of the adequate rendering of any thought in translation into any language. The author himself later solves this contradiction by subdividing the translation process into two categories: restricted translation and total translation, which could be rebaptized "microtranslation" and "macrotranslation." The first category covers the translation of lexical units and grammatical forms; the second category covers what is traditionally known as "shifts," or translations from one level of language into another and from one category into another. We have every right to classify these "transitions" as translational transformations, whether or not we accept the theory of levels of language, which has been rightly criticized of late (Kacnel'son 1972). After all, translation takes place in the sphere of parole, and it is by no means obligated to make use of interlanguage correspondences. Catford himself arrives at this salutary conclusion, neutralizing all the obstacles he set up in his earlier argument, by stating that every equivalent translation "should relate to one and the same essence" (1965: 72). If we substitute "segment of reality" for the vague notion of "essence" we find ourselves in perfect agreement with him.

Yet even though the whole, Catford's "macrotranslation," takes precedence over its parts, translators still remain under the obligation to render not just *what* is said in the original, but also *how* it has been said. Translators must therefore go through a stage of analysis in the translation process. If we were to limit ourselves to macrotranslation only and if we were to apply a deductive method, we could never speak of the equivalence of every means chosen by the translator for rendering the original's expressive and stylistic peculiarities. Without a careful, meticulous analysis of the original's linguistic devices no adequate recreation of the unity of form and content is possible in translation. That is why we must pay so much attention to "microtranslation" and to lexical correspondences, equivalents, and variants.

VARIANT CORRESPONDENCES

Variant correspondences are established between words when the target language offers several words to render one and the same meaning of a source language word. The noun "soldier," for instance, has at least four correspondences in Russian: "soldat," "ryadovoi," "voennosluzhashtii," "voennyi." But this does not allow us to label "soldier" a polysemantic word. Even in the – quite numerous – cases when Russian correspondences are not synonymous, this does not allow us to label the corresponding French or English word polysemantic. In fact, many lexical units in those two languages are non-differentiated, that is, they express a general notion not expressed by just one word in Russian. They often express abstract notions. The *Big English–Russian Dictionary* lists four equivalents for the noun "sincerity," namely "iskrennost'," "chistoserdechie," "pryamota," and "chestnost'." "Sincerity" 's French analog, "sincérité" can also be rendered by "iskrennost'" and "chistoserdechie." The adjective "sincere," however, is given eight meanings in the big dictionary, namely: "(1) iskrennyi, nepoddel'nyi; (2) istinnyi, podlinnyi, nastoyashtii; (3) pryamoi, chestnyi, provednyi." These meanings are illustrated by means of expressions such as "a sincere friend," translated as "istinnyi (nastoyashtii) drug," and "a sincere life," rendered as "chestnaya (pravednaya) zhizn'." This allows us to conclude that all eight Russian equivalents are mere variants of the lexical meaning of the word "sincere," that they are its variant correspondences.

The variant correspondences that consist of Russian synonyms derived from the same root are perhaps the most important feature of the relationship between the vocabularies of Russian and English. Let us just take the words that correspond to the English adjective "flying": "letayushtii," "letatel'nyi," "letnyi," "letuchii," as in "letayushtie tarelki" or "flying saucer," "letatel'nyi aparat" or "flying machine," "letnaya pogioda" or "breezy weather," and "Letuchii Gollandec" or "The Flying Dutchman." The word "flying" itself is by no means polysemantic, of course, and the point is that Russian uses more differentiated adjectives than English does, depending on the noun that is defined.

It would be wrong to assume that the numerous cases of

differentiation of meaning in translation from English to Russian provide sufficient arguments in favor of the opinion that in Russian the more detailed and concrete meaning prevails in all cases over the more general one. On the contrary: some of the most widely used Russian adjectives have two English equivalents. "Bol'shoj," for instance, can be both "big" and "large"; "malen'kij" can be both "little" and "small"; and "vysokij" can be both "high" and "tall." The same phenomenon occurs in the case of nouns. "Etazh" is both "floor" and "storey," and "gryaz" is "dirt," "filth," and "mud." The latter are, of course, not fully synonymous. Rather, they refer to one and the same general notion, but each of them has a specific secondary distinguishing feature that reveals itself when they are used in standard expressions. "Filth," for instance, has the figurative meaning of moral decay.

CONTEXTUAL MEANING AND TRANSLATION

Contextual meanings appear when a word is actually functioning in a concrete speech/parole situation, in specific surroundings. Contextual meanings are realized under the influence of the narrow, the wider, and the extralinguistic context. Frequency of occurrence allows us to distinguish between *usual* (repeated) and *occasional* (chance) contextual meanings. As time passes and observation adds its weight to observation, the former join the set of variant correspondences while the latter appear and disappear as manifestations of subjective language use on the part of different authors. They are to be encountered mainly in fiction.

The conversion of a word from the category "occasional" to the category "usual" is one of the most common factors in the development of polysemy. There are many reasons why speakers may decide to abandon the generally accepted word that suggests itself automatically to them and to substitute another word for it, used in a less traditional manner. This substitution may be caused by a sudden association of ideas, a moment of affectation, an urge for expressive loading, an attempt to achieve a comic effect, or simply a desire to attract the listener's attention. Translators obviously need to pay attention not just to such an unusual use of words but also to the reason or reasons for it.

Contextual meanings are not always introduced from outside. Rather, they represent the realization of some semantic element potentially contained in the meaning of a word and foregrounded by the wider context – a neighboring sentence, for instance, or the whole. This dependence is demonstrated very clearly when synonyms of different intensity are used in the source language, and when the translator decides to keep the same relationship between the Russian synonyms.

Consider, for instance: "The owners of the presses have taken the point made by the Tories and for many years the noisy presses of Fleet Street have skilfully maintained an almost total silence on Irish affairs. It was an effective blackout." The translation reads: "Magnaty pressy usvoili tochku zreniya konservatorov, i na protyazhenii mnogih let kriklivye organy pechati Flit-strit ne obmolvilis' ni slovom o polozhenii v Severnoi Irlandii. Eto byl nastoyashtij zagovor molchaniya." The variant "hranili molchanie o polozenii v Irlandii" would have been quite acceptable, but even so the word "blackout" would have needed a stronger equivalent than "molchanie" in the translation. "Blackout" is being used in a growing variety of meanings in English, but the one it has in this particular case was fixed for the first time in the Russian dictionaries of the 1960s as "zasekrechivanie, cenzurnyi zapret," or "blackout," "suppression of news." The point of the text under discussion, however, is the unofficial decision on the part of the newspaper owners to keep quiet about the critical situation in Ireland. The Russian translator has seen fit to translate that decision as "zagovor," or "plot." This contextual exposition of the meaning of the word has been achieved by means of expressive concretization, and it can be justified or rejected only after a stylistic analysis of the whole article.

OBJECTIVE SITUATION AND SPEECH SITUATION

The most important constituents of the so-called extralinguistic context are the objective setting and the speech situation, as defined by Gak: by objective setting is meant the time and place of utterance. The objective setting (or, as Gak calls it, situation) involves "the objective relationships: the objects and their interaction depicted in the utterance" (1969: 20). The speech situation, on the other hand, is defined as "the situation and the conditions of the communication, the attitude the speaker exhibits towards the addressee, the surroundings they both find themselves in, and the general goal of the utterance" (Gak 1969: 19).

An important element of the objective setting is the country that is the subject of the utterance. In his book *Only Yesterday*, for instance, F. Allen describes the facts that cars have ousted all other means of transportation as follows: "the interurban trolley perished, or survived only as a pathetic anachronism." The British "trolley" would become "troleibus" in Russian, but there are no "troleibusy" in the USA, nor have there ever been. If the utterance containing the word "trolley" were to be set in the USA, therefore, "trolley" would have to become "tramvai" in Russian.

To establish the meaning of the word "abolitionist," to take another example, translators should know both the country and the epoch in which it is used. The *Big English–Russian Dictionary* translates "abolitionist" as "abolitionist," but explains: "storonnik otmeny, uprazdneniya (zakona i tomu podobnomu)." How should we translate "abolitionist" referring to Al Smith, the Republican Party's candidate in the 1928 elections? In the USA of the 1920s the word could only refer to the abolition of the "dry laws."

The name of Sidney Silverston often appeared in the British press of the 1950s and 1960s. He was referred to as the oldest abolitionist in the House of Commons, meaning the oldest living supporter of the abolition of capital punishment in the United Kingdom, and the man who had drafted the law designed to indeed abolish it. Translators who are not familiar with the situation would be at a loss to translate the word.

Summing up, a speech situation consists of the following components: (i) it reflects the personality of the author or speaker; (ii) it reflects the source in which the original has been published; (iii) it reflects the addressee for whom the utterance is meant; and (iv) it reflects the purpose of the translation, the expected effect it is supposed to have on the reader or listener.

All these components of the speech situation go beyond the boundaries of the text, but every single one of them can be expressed by means of linguistic devices, at least to some degree. In drama, for instance, the elements of the speech situation include not only *what* characters say, but also *how* they say it. In a number of plays by George Bernard Shaw the utterances of the characters matter much more than their actions, and full understanding of the characters therefore requires full command of the context, or even subtext, which is represented to a considerable extent by the speech situation. Shaw himself was well aware of this, since he supplements some of his plays by introductions hardly much shorter than the plays themselves. It is obvious that elements taken from the theory of literature must be included in an analysis of the speech situation.

W. Foster writes in an article about the crash of 1929: "The period of apparent prosperity may be said to have ended in 1928." The adjective "apparent" can have one of two diametrically opposed meanings: either "ochevidnyi, yavnyi," or "kazhushtiisya, mnimyi." What kind of prosperity does the text refer to? The author never mentions the word again, and so the answer can be found only in the extralinguistic context. The author's personality reveals itself as the factor that will help translators make the correct decision. Foster was the secretary general of the US Communist Party, and he would hardly have considered the prosperity of the Coolidge years "real," if only because the army of the unemployed topped 1 million by the time Coolidge left the White House. We are therefore completely justified in translating the sentence as: "mozhno skazat', chto period mnimogo protsvetania zakonchilsya v 1928 godu."

The importance of the source in which the original is published may be illustrated by means of translations of texts taken from the British newspaper the *Guardian*, which used to support the Liberal Party. Like the party itself, the newspaper used to occupy the middle ground between Labour and the Conservatives. It would therefore occasionally criticize both, but without offering a distinct enough program of its own. An article on Britain's joining the Common Market reaches the following conclusion: "the political parties must consider again the nature of the public interest in this transformed economy." This is an utterance which looks like an equation with two unknowns, since "public interest" and "transformed economy" could be interpreted both as "gosudarstvennyi interest" and "vygoda dlya naseleniya," respectively, and as "preobrazovannaya ekonomika," which is rather vague, and "nacionalizirovannuyu chast narodnogo hozyaistva." If we take into account the general tone of the editorial as well as the general tendency of the liberal press to maneuver between its two stronger opponents, we should give preference to the more vague translation.

The importance of the role of the addressee may be illustrated by the following example. It was not uncommon to see President Nixon referred to as "Richard" or even "Dick" in American newspapers. This is totally unacceptable in Russian translation because it sounds far too familiar. A correction is therefore necessary in the translation, not only because it reflects the proper attitude towards the person referred to, but also because it represents an adequate rendering of the impact of the utterance on the original reader.

Extralinguistic factors are extremely important for the translation of nicknames and curses. In *To Kill a Mockingbird*, Harper Lee's novel, the little girl is called "Scout" on the analogy of "boy scout," or "razvedchitsa." The Russian "razvedchitsa" would not correspond to the girl's appearance and character at all, and the translators have consequently called her "Glazastik."

Two final examples will illustrate the impact of the setting on the reader of the translation. In the Russian translation of F. Scott Fitzgerald's *The Great Gatsby* we read: "Ya okonchil Yeilskii universitet v 1915 godu." The same sentence in the original reads: "I graduated from New Haven in 1915," without any mention of Yale. A literal translation like "Ya okonchil vysshee uchebnoe zavedenie v Nyu-Heivene" would not mean anything to the average Russian reader. The translator (E. Kalashnikova) therefore preferred the concrete name of the university, the more so since Yale, established in 1702, is the oldest American university. For the average US reader the geographical name New Haven is undoubtedly "socially established and contextualized" as associated with Yale University. Kalashnikova's substitution is aimed at the production of an analogous reception on the part of the Russian reader.

The importance of the socially established context can be illustrated by means of another example from the work of the same author and the same translator. *Tender is the Night* has the sentence: "The chauffeur, a Russian czar of the period of Ivan the Terrible...." A literal translation would obviously be absurd: what other czars could there possibly have been at the time of Ivan the Terrible except, precisely, Ivan the Terrible. Besides, a chauffeur's outward appearance could hardly resemble that of a royal personage. For the American reader the word "czar" obviously has connotations different from those evoked for the Russian reader by the corresponding Russian word. Here, too, the correction of the "socially established context" seems fully justifiable.

WORKS CITED

Bol'shoj anglo–russkij slovar' [*Big English–Russian Dictionary*], ed. I. Gal'perin, compiled by N. Amossova *et al.*, Moscow: Sovetskaya entsiclopediya, 1972.

Catford, J. (1965) *A Linguistic Theory of Translation*, Oxford: Oxford University Press.

Gak, V. (1969) "O modelyah yazykovogo sinteza" [On the models of language synthesis], *Inostrannye yazyki v shkole* [*Foreign Language Teaching in Schools*] No. 4, Moscow.

Kacnel'son, S. (1972) *Tipologiya yazyka i rechevoe myshlenie* [*Language Typology and Thinking in Speech*], Leningrad: Nauka.

Chapter 4

Interlanguage asymmetry and the prognostication of transformations in translation

Vladimir Gak

This essay represents a different strand in the Russian and Bulgarian tradition: the pedagogical one. Translation pedagogy is different from what it is in the West, where it was until recently ghettoized inside the "workshop" in most educational institutions. In many cases, that workshop would profess to deal with translation and translations while in fact catering to the wishes and desires of the frustrated creative writers participating in it, often with minimal competence in any language not their own.

This level of dilettantism has long been left behind in the study and teaching of translation in Russia and Bulgaria, precisely because the critical vocabulary has been stabilized and the level of analysis is higher, less speculative, and less inclined to pay undue attention to what prospective translators "feel." In fact, translation pedagogy may be said to be situated on a level between what is known as "the workshop" and "the theory class" in the West.

In such a situation, it becomes relevant for the teacher to be interested in "prognostication." If a conceptual scheme can be developed that is able to predict at what point students are likely to experience difficulties, teachers can make use of this prognostication to prepare their students (and their classes) accordingly. The difficulties can be seen as belonging to a logical progression in the process of translation, and they need not unduly disturb the student of that process. In fact, this way of initiating students to the translation process is likely to increase their confidence, both in themselves and in the subject they are studying.

A. L.

In philosophy symmetry is defined as a category denoting the process of existence and the establishing of identical features under given conditions and in certain relations. In its dynamic aspect symmetry reveals itself in a definite interaction between certain physical elements: it appears whenever an element A presupposes the appearance of an element B. Any deviation from this kind of regular correspondence results in asymmetry. From this point of view the notions of symmetry and asymmetry in language can be applied not only to the relationships obtaining between signifier and signified within a certain language, but also to interlanguage relationships between two signifiers, as in the case of translation.

In translation a confrontation takes place between units of two different languages. These units can be of two types in their relationship to each other.

(1) **Isomorphous units** have identical meaning or are characterized by identical positions in the corresponding language systems. Examples are the French words "homme," "pomme," "table," "prendre," "blanc" [man, apple, table, take, white] and the Russian words "chelovek," "yabloko," "stol," "brat'," "belyj." Polysemy does not undermine isomorphism. The relationships pomme–apple and homme–man will still be considered isomorphous.

Isomorphous relationships also obtain between some grammatical categories, such as the infinitive, the participle, the present tense, the singular and the plural, the masculine and the feminine gender of animate nouns in Russian, German, and French. Isomorphous units constitute interlanguage systemic equivalents.

(2) **Allomorphous units** do not correspond to systemic equivalents in the other language. They can be divided into two groups:
   (a) lexical or grammatical lacunae, as when a grammatical category is not present in one of the languages, or when there is no separate unit available for a certain meaning – well-known examples are the absence in West European languages of the category of "aspect" so characteristic of Russian verbs, or the absence of the definite article in Russian;
   (b) a difference in the semantic volume of some words or grammatical categories. The French verbs "mettre" and "remplir" ["put" and "fill"] not only correspond to the verbs "klast" or "napolnjat" in Russian, but also to "sypat'," "lit'," "nasypat'," and "nalivat'," since the choice of the Russian verb denoting

the corresponding action depends on the nature of the substance (liquid, solid, or powdery) being poured. On the other hand, several French grammatical forms correspond to the single form of the Russian past tense.

Equivalence in translation is based on systemic interlanguage equivalents that constitute symmetrical correspondences. In the case of translation, however, it is often necessary to neglect systemic equivalents and to resort to translational transformations, in which elements that are not structurally symmetrical play the part of functional equivalents.

The matching of structural and translational equivalents results in "word for word" translation, or interlanguage symmetry, while the difference between them results in interlanguage asymmetry, "free" or "transformed" translation.

Like any other process, translational transformation can be studied with reference to the conditions that generate it, its types and variations, and its pragmatic results. Translation theory is more obviously interested in the study of types of translational transformations. It is interested in the concrete analysis of the conditions under which transformations occur, and of the elements that constitute those transformations. The question then arises: Can these elements be presented in a generalized manner? This question is also of primary importance for the practice of translation, since the formulation of general conditions that make it necessary to eschew word for word translation will make it possible to prognosticate translational transformations and to foresee when word for word translation is possible and when it has to be abandoned.

We can speak of translational transformations in the strict sense of the term only when the translator has refrained from using the isomorphous units that exist in both languages. The problem of rendering lexico-grammatical units to which no equivalents, or only partial equivalents, correspond in the target language has been sufficiently covered by both general and language-pair specific theories of translation, and I shall therefore not discuss it here. It is worth mentioning, though, that the move from the more abstract to the more concrete unit is by no means straightforward in cases in which the semantic volumes of two languages only partially overlap. Rather, in these cases the move from abstract to concrete tends to take place in two stages. If the Russian word "ruka," for instance, corresponds in some West European languages to lexical units with a more concrete meaning, such as "bras" or "main" in French, or "arm" and "hand" in English, this most emphatically does not mean that the move from abstract to concrete occurs only in the direction from Russian and towards French and English; nor is a word with a narrower meaning always substituted for a word with a broader meaning in translations from these two languages into Russian. Rather, it is often the case that the more concrete words in French and English correspond to even more concrete words in Russian, such as "plecho" or "lokot'." Similarly, there is no article in Russian, but this fact does not mean that the article used in West European languages always corresponds to a zero determinative in Russian. On the contrary, the definite and indefinite articles used in West European languages often correspond to more concrete determinatives in Russian, such as "etot," "moj," "takoj," "kakoj-to," "kakoj-nibud'," among others. The move from abstract to concrete can therefore be said to take place not just from language 1 to language 2, but also from language 2 to language 1.

We should consider only the abandonment of systemic equivalents based on isomorphous elements in a language as translational transformations *par excellence*. Transformations are conditioned by interlanguage asymmetry on the syntagmatic, paradigmatic, or semiotic level.

Asymmetry on the syntagmatic level reduces to a lack of correspondence between the number of signifieds and signifiers in the chain of speech. Therefore, we have every reason to prognosticate a non-word-for-word (or free) translation whenever a given notion can be expressed by means of a combination of two lexical units in one of a pair of languages. In Russian and in French, for instance, one and the same notion, "progulyat'sya" [to stroll], can be expressed both by a single word and by a combination of words. We therefore get the possible pairing of "progulyat'sya/se promener" and of "sovershat' progulku/faire une promenade" [go for a stroll]. This makes it possible to use asymmetry in translation. One word in one language can be made to correspond to an expression in another language, as in "Oni zahoteli nemnogo progulyat'sya po gorodu" [they wanted to stroll a little in town] and "Ils ont voulu faire une petite promenade en ville" [they wanted to take a little stroll in town].

A particular case of syntagmatic asymmetry is arbitrary mutual conditioning, a phrase first used by Charles Bally to denote the mutual dependence obtaining in the choice between the forms of two syntagmatically related elements. This often occurs in the translation of semi-free combinations. Russian "prochitat' lekciyu" [to read a lecture], for instance, corresponds to French "faire une conférence" [make a lecture]. Similarly, Russian "udelit' vnimanie" corresponds to English "pay attention." The deviation from the systemic equivalents "chitat'/lire" and "platit'/pay" is conditioned by the rules of co-occurrence connected with the neighboring words.

In the case of paradigmatic asymmetry, on the other hand, deviation from systemic equivalence is governed by the following rule: if the linguistic units are used in their primary functions, translational transformations are not only not obligatory, but often even impossible. If, on the other hand, linguistic units appear in non-obligatory or non-primary usage, translational transformations are not only possible, but also often obligatory. If a linguistic unit has been used in a secondary function, this serves as a signal for a possible, or even obligatory, transformation on the translator's part.

The primary function is the initial function for which a certain linguistic unit has been created. It is always meaningful and can be demonstrated in opposition to other units. Secondary functions, on the other hand, can be divided into three types: (i) neutralization, in which the basic distinctive features of the poles of the opposition are nullified; (ii) transposition, in which one of the poles of the opposition is used in the function normally reserved for the other; and (iii) desemantization, in which a given unit loses its own meaning.

Neutralization occurs when the opposition between A and B is nullified and A signifies a general notion C. Transposition occurs when A is used in the meaning of B, and desemantization occurs when A loses its meaning. In any of these cases A is not necessarily translated into the target language by means of its isomorphous correspondent A' in that language.

Neutralization occurs in the following examples. If the verb "pridti" in a Russian phrase has been used in the general meaning of "to come," the opposition between the semes "on foot" and "using a vehicle" that distinguishes this verb from the verb "priehat' " need not be rendered in translation, and "On uzhe prishel" simply becomes "Il est déjà arrivé" [he has already come]. If, on the other hand, the verb "pridti" functions as the desemantized component of a verbal noun phrase in which it signals the acquisition of a certain state or quality by the subject, it can be translated in various ways, or the whole phrase can be rendered by means of a single verb. "Pridti na smenu" can be rendered as "faire la relève" [to take over], "Pridti v otchayanie" can be rendered as "tomber dans le désespoir" [to fall into despair], and "pridti v negodovanie" can be rendered as "s'indigner" [to become indignant].

The phrases "il a vu un chien" [he has seen a dog] and "Il regarde le chien de son voisin" [he is looking at his neighbor's dog] will be rendered by a definite or an indefinite article in any language that possesses those articles. But when a given proposition refers to the whole class of the objects mentioned the opposition between definiteness and indefiniteness is nullified. Since there are no specialized linguistic forms to be used for this generalized meaning, one of the poles of the opposition definite–indefinite is used in that function – which becomes a secondary function for it. Usually the unmarked pole (the indefinite article) is used in this way, but the marked pole can also be used. As with any other transfer, the choice of the unit to be used in its non-primary function is every language's "internal affair." Therefore, a generalized meaning can be translated by means of allomorphous units, which may give rise to lexical and grammatical differences. English, for instance, uses the indefinite article far more often than French or Spanish to express generalized meaning. Thus English has "A dog is an animal," using the indefinite article twice, whereas French and Spanish have "Le chien est un animal" and "El perro es un animal" respectively, each using one definite and one indefinite article.

In cases of neutralization French usually resorts to the singular and Russian to the plural, as is obvious from the translation of the following sentence from Saint-Exupéry: "L'homme se découvre quand il se mesure avec l'obstacle. Mais pour l'atteindre il lui faut un outil" [Man discovers himself when he measures himself against an obstacle. But to reach it he needs a tool] as "Chelovek poznaet sebya v bor'be s prepyatstviyami. No dlya etoi bor'by emu nuzhny orudiya."

Most languages use the present tense to refer to concrete actions occurring simultaneously with the utterance. But to express an event out of time (and therefore in the function of neutralization) Russian uses forms of the past or future tenses more often than French or English. Compare "Deux et deux font quatre" [Two and two make four] with "Dva i dva (budet) chetyre."

The following is an example of transposition. The so-called historical present (the use of the present tense to refer to past actions) is more characteristic for Russian than for French. Thus the

French *présent historique* is often translated by an allomorphous linguistic unit in Russian, namely the past tense. If the present tense is used in its primary function, it can be translated by means of a present tense; if it is used in a secondary function translational transformations are much more likely.

Translational transformations are even more likely in cases of desemantization. *Pluralia tanta,* for instance, have been desemantized, and it is therefore no coincidence that we discover many differences in their translation from one language to another. The Russian "vesy," "chernila," "arkhiv," "gerb," for example, correspond to the French "balance," "encre," "archives," "armes" [scale, ink, archive, arms].

Asymmetry occurs on the semiotic level when a signified denoted in one language does not have a signifier in another. This mainly occurs in the case of redundant usage of lexemes in one of the languages. Lexemes tend to have a structural formal function in such usage. The redundancy of words and grammatical forms is caused by two factors: context and situation. Compare the following sentences: "Des soldats coiffés de casques lourds, chaussés de grosses bottes" [Soldiers wearing heavy helmets and big boots] and "Soldaty v tyazhelyh kaskah i grubyh sapogah." The French past participles are redundant since their meaning is presupposed by the nouns that follow them. They have the structural function of linking one of the nouns to the other. This same function is performed by prepositions in Russian. In this way "the superfluous sign ceases to signify," to quote Wittgenstein, and it can be removed from the text without detriment to the content.

Exactly the same phenomenon occurs when a word points to something already made obvious by the situation. Compare the well-known phrases "Ponyatno?/Vous avez compris?" [Did you understand?] and "Mozhno voiti?/Je peux entrer?" [Can I come in?]. Unlike their French counterparts, the Russian sentences contain no markers identifying listeners or speakers.

Let me repeat, in conclusion, that translational transformations are often caused either by the use of words or grammatical forms in their secondary functions (as in the case of neutralization, transposition, and desemantization) or by textual or situational redundance. On the other hand, whenever linguistic units are necessary, and therefore used in their primary functions, they can be translated by means of isomorphous units as long as such units exist in the target language.

Chapter 5
The problem of the unit of translation

Leonid Barkhudarov

Much has been written on the "problem" of the unit of translation, probably because the concept of such a unit is potentially interesting for translation pedagogy. If students of translation could be told how to cut up texts and which pieces to replace with which other pieces, they could, once again, be programmed in such a way that they would produce "good" translations.

The nostalgia for man as the perfect translation machine, which haunts so much writing on translation down to the present, can easily be shown to be the point of departure for any search for any kind of viable "unit" of translation.

It has become obvious by now that the old notion of "equivalence" on the level of the word, the sentence (viewed as a cumulative addition of words), or the text (viewed as a cumulative addition of sentences) is simply not enough. To translate one has to know languages; to translate well one has to go beyond languages. To train translators one has to teach them languages; to train them well one has to take them beyond languages.

All of this strongly suggests that the elusive "unit" of translation is, in fact, the communicative situation described above, and very little else. The basic decision that translators make on how to tackle their texts is therefore made on that level and no other.

This is, of course, the very level that is not easy to describe, categorize, and formalize, the level where the translators' creativity is very much in evidence. It is not inconceivable, therefore, that the acknowledgment of the "communicative situation" as the unit of translation also entails the admission that the translators' primordial decision will always be "creative," rather than "scientific," with the proviso that translators will be able to make the most potentially productive "creative" decision on the basis of the most relevant "scientific" information available to them.

A. L.

Translation is the process of transformation of a speech product (or text) produced in one language into a speech product (or text) in another language. During this process of transformation the level of content should remain unchanged. This implies that substitution does take place on the level of expression, or language units, whereas on the level of content, the information contained in the text, everything remains intact or, to be more precise, relatively unchanged. It follows that the most important task of the translator who carries out the process of transformation, and of the theorist who describes or creates a model for that process, is to establish the minimal unit of translation or, as it is generally called, the unit of translation in the source text. Roganova has called this unit a "transleme" (1971: 30). We have to bear in mind that the term "unit of translation" is not a very precise one. It would be more correct to speak of a "unit of translational equivalence" of a source language unit that corresponds to an equivalent in the text of the translation.

The problem of the unit of translation ranks among the most complicated problems of translation theory. Many views have been expressed on the subject, including one that rejects the very possibility of its existence. It is also not clear what criteria should be used for establishing the unit of translation. Nor is it clear on what basis such a unit should be established: units taken from the source language or from the target language? elements of linguistic form (structure) or content? and we could go on. Komissarov provides us with a survey of these different points of view (1973: 185–90). In what follows I shall limit myself to developing my own position.

I define "unit of translation" as "a unit in the source text for which an equivalent can be found in the text of the translation but whose elements, taken separately, do not correspond to equivalents in the translated text." In other words, the unit of translation is the *minimal* language unit in the source text that corresponds to an equivalent in the target text. As we shall see later, it can have a very complicated structure and it can even consist of smaller units of the source language, but none of these sub-units, taken separately, is "translatable": it is impossible to find equivalents for them in the text of the translation, even when they have comparatively independent meanings of their own in the source language.

Linguistics considers the morpheme as the smallest meaningful unit of language. Even so, morphemes very rarely play the part of units of translation. The integral, indivisible meaning is more often than not carried by a language unit of a higher level (a word, for instance, a combination of words, or even a sentence), and not by any morpheme. Even in cases where these higher level units can be semantically divided, that is, when their components (including morphemes) have meanings of their own, their equivalent in the target language often turns out to be an indivisible unit. This unit does not have elements as its components that are equivalent to those in the source language unit. The unit is then again not the morpheme, and often not even the word or combination of words, but the whole "higher" unit of the source language.

The unit of translation can be a unit on any of the levels of language. Let us therefore first describe these levels, as distinguished by contemporary linguistics. We can list the levels of the phoneme (grapheme in writing), the morpheme, the word, the combination of words, the sentence, the text. The latter has not yet been universally accepted, but it is necessary for any analysis of translation, since translation deals with speech (or parole) and the concrete speech products (or texts), rather than with language as a system (or langue).

The phoneme (and its written equivalent, the grapheme or letter symbol) is not supposed to carry a separate meaning: it only distinguishes between various meanings. Nevertheless, phonemes or graphemes may function as units of translation when target language phonemes similar in articulation and acoustic qualities are substituted for source language phonemes, or when target language graphemes symbolizing similar sounds are substituted for source language graphemes. To render the English last name "Heath," for instance, the translator must select a Russian phoneme to correspond to each of the English ones, that is, phonemes close enough to English in articulation and sound. This type of translation, in which equivalence has been established on the level of the phoneme, is called translational (or practical) transcription. If equivalence is established on the level of the grapheme, that is, if the translator has not rendered the sound of the source word but its graphic representation, the result of the transformation process is called "translational transliteration," as when English "Lincoln" is translated into Russian as "Linkol'n." In practice strict distinctions between transcriptions and transliterations hardly occur. Rather, translators usually opt for a combination of the two. "Newton," for instance, becomes "N'yuton" in Russian, an obvious mixture of transcription and transliteration, since the proper transcription would be "N'yuten" and the proper transliteration "Nevton," which is exactly the way his name appears in eighteenth-century Russian translations.

Translation occurs on the level of the phoneme and the grapheme mainly in the rendering of names of people and places, or of different types of political and ethnic realia. "Brain drain," for instance, becomes "brein drein" in Russian, and the "speaker" of the House of Commons becomes "spiker." Needless to say, translation on the level of the phoneme and grapheme is so limited precisely because neither the phoneme nor the grapheme carries meaning.

Translations such as "speaker/spiker" or "lady/ledi" are probably no longer considered translations on the phonemic level. Since words of this type have entered the lexicon of the Russian language, the choice of equivalent takes place on the level of the word, at least from the translator's point of view. Translators pick up dictionary equivalents for units of the English text, no matter whether they render the pronunciation of the source word or its written form. Only when translators are faced with the lack of a "ready" equivalent and are therefore forced to create an "occasional translational equivalent," which makes them resort to transcription, are they using the phoneme as a unit of translation. Yet we must keep in mind that there is no strictly defined boundary between "speech" equivalents and "occasional" equivalents. We are also interpreting the notion "process of translation" here in its purely linguistic sense, that of a definite interlanguage transformation, that is, a transformation of a text in the source language into a text in the target language, without taking the psycholinguistic aspect of the process, that is, the translator's own activity, into account.

In the case of "speaker/spiker," therefore, the equivalence is established on the level of the word from the translator's point of view, even though the theorist of translation will maintain that equivalence exists on the level of the phoneme. This also holds for analogous cases on other levels of language. The theorist will treat the translation of "backbencher" as "zadneskameechnik" or of "House of Commons" as "palata obshtin" as translation on the level of the morpheme and on the level of the word respectively. If the translator, on the other hand, resorts to ready equivalents, the unit of translation will be the word in the first case, the combination of words in the second.

In some cases the unit of translation turns out to be the morpheme. Each of the morphemes of the source word corresponds to an equivalent in the corresponding word in the target language. such correspondences can be observed in the pairing of English "tables" and Russian "stoly." The Russian root "stol" corresponds to the root of the English "table," and the Russian plural marker "y" corresponds to the English plural marker "s." Translation on the level of the morpheme is even more rare than translation on the level of the phoneme or grapheme since the morphological structure of semantically equivalent words is usually very different in different languages, especially in the case of word-formatives and grammatical morphemes.

The word appears much more often as a unit of translation. Russian "On prishel domoi," for instance, corresponds to English "He came home." This correspondence is based on the word as unit of translation; it could not possibly be based on the phoneme/grapheme, or on the morpheme. We must remind ourselves at this point that when we refer to "units of translation" we mean units of the source language. We are therefore justified in speaking of translation on the level of the word even in cases where more than one word in the target language corresponds to just one word in the source language. J. D. Salinger's sentence "Jane and her mother were sort of snubbing her" has been translated into Russian as "Dzhein i ee mat' otnosyatsya k nei svysoka." The Russian idiom "otnosyatsya svysoka" corresponds to the English word "snub." Yet we are still dealing with translation on the level of the word because the target language idiom corresponds to the source language word. In cases like these (which are quite numerous) we may speak of "interlevel equivalents." The source language unit of translation has been rendered into the target language by a unit that belongs to another, usually higher, level (although the opposite also occurs). In cases where the unit of translation and its target language equivalent belong to the same level of language we may speak of "unilevel equivalents."

Translations on the level of the word are much more common than translations on the level of the language, but their distribution is also limited. As a rule, only some of the words in any given sentence will correspond to words in the target language. The translation of the rest of the sentence is usually achieved on a higher level: that of the combination of words. Word for word translation is usually possible only for very simple and short sentences like the one quoted above. Different types of grammatical constraints as well as lexical factors make it impossible, or very difficult, to translate more or less complex sentences on the level of the word.

The most typical example of translation on the level of the combination of words is the translation of idiomatic or phraseological units. As is well known, the meaning of such units is not that of the sum total of their components, which is why it is impossible to translate them word for word in most cases, and why the idiom or phrase plays the part of the unit of translation. English "to catch fire" cannot be translated into Russian word for word. Rather, it corresponds to a unit like "zagoret'sya."

It should not be assumed, though, that idioms and phraseological phrases are the only possible translation units on the level of the combination of words. Sometimes such a unit can be a free combination of words, whose source language meaning is built up out of the meanings of its separate components, as in English "to come late" translated into Russian as "opozdat'." Every separate word in English has retained its dictionary meaning, but the role of the unit of translation for translation into Russian is performed by the whole combination. Another example could be "I improved her game immensely," translated into Russian as "No ya ee zdorovo natreniroval." "Improved her game" is the unit of translation since its word components have no word equivalents in Russian; equivalence can be achieved only on the level of the combination of words taken as a whole.

Translation on the level of the combination of words is very common. Very often part of a sentence is translated on the level of the word and the rest on the level of the combination of words. A sentence like "The terrestrial globe is a member of the solar system," translated as "Zemnoi shar vhodit v solnechnuyu sistemu," is a case in point. The following correspondences can be established on the level of the word: "terrestrial/zemnoi," "globe/shar," "solar/solnechnuyu," and "system/sistemu." "Is a member of," on the other hand, is rendered on the level of the combination of words: "vhodit v."

In some cases even combinations of words cannot serve as units of translation; only the sentence can. Once again, this usually happens when the overall meaning of a sentence is not the sum total of the meanings of the words and combinations of words that it consists of, as in proverbs like "Net huda bez dobra," translated as

Problem of the unit of translation 45

"Every cloud has a silver lining." Clichés, such as "Keep off the grass," translated as "Po gazonam ne hodit'," are also translated in this manner.

Finally, there are cases in which even the sentence cannot be used as a unit of translation, and such a unit turns out to be the whole text of the original, that is, the whole group of independent sentences integrated into the framework of that single fragment of speech. Such cases are undoubtedly very rare in prose, but they are quite common in the translation of poetry.

The concept "level of translation" can, in my opinion, be connected with such current concepts of translation theory as "equivalent," "adequate," "literal," and "free" translation. Generally speaking, the concept of translation equivalence evidently does not reduce only to the choice of the necessary unit of translation on one level of language or another, but the correct choice of this unit on the right level of language is undoubtedly of primary importance in every concrete case.

A translation made on a level both necessary and sufficient for the adequate rendering of the level of content without violating the norms of the target language is an equivalent translation.

A translation made on a level lower than the one necessary for the preservation of the level of content combined with a parallel preservation of the norms of the target language is a literal translation. If we were to translate the phrase "is a member" in the sentence quoted above as "yavlyaetcya chlenom," we would have made a literal translation, because according to the norms of the Russian language it would be more proper to render this expression on a higher level, namely that of the combination of words, as in "vhodit v." Similarly, if we were to translate "Keep off the grass" as "Derzhite proch'ot travy," we would again have made a literal translation because we would have chosen the word as the unit of translation. The norms of the Russian language, however, require that the whole sentence function as the unit of translation, as in "Po gazonam ne hodit'." Literal translation is not admissible because it deforms either the content of the information communicated in the source text, or the norms of the target language, or both. Literal translations should therefore be considered mistakes made by the translator, as when English "cold-blooded murder" is translated on the morphemic level as "hladno[cold]krov[blood]n[ed]oe." The correct rendering is to be found on the level of the word, as in "zverskoe ubiistvo." Another example is the translation of a "regular ass" as "regulyarnyi osel." This translation is made on the level of the word instead of on the higher level of the combination of words, where the correct Russian equivalent is to be found in "kruglyi durak."

A translation made on a level higher than the one required for an exhaustive rendering of the contents of the source text according to the norms of the target language is a free translation, as when "Some things are hard to remember" is translated as "Byvaet, chto nipochem ne mozhesh vspomnit', kak vse bylo." The translation has been made on the sentence level, that is, the source English sentence has been rendered as an integral unit, whereas it is quite possible to produce a translation "much closer to the text," as the saying goes, that is, on the level of the combination of words, or even of the word itself.

Free translations are, on the whole, more acceptable than literal ones, since they are able to preserve both the sense of the original and the norms of the target language better. Their negative side is that they can lead to considerable loss of information as a result of far-reaching changes in the source text that are not always necessary and can often be avoided. Needless to say, free translations are not preferable in all cases. Rather, their use depends on the generic character of the original. Thus free translation is quite common and acceptable in the translation of literary texts, but it cannot be tolerated in the translation of juridical and diplomatic documents. The translator's goal is always to achieve equivalence, no matter what type of text is translated. In practice, though, it is very hard to classify translations as either equivalent or non-equivalent. It would therefore be more correct to speak of different degrees of equivalence, with absolute equivalence more likely to remain an ideal than ever to become a reality.

WORKS CITED

Komissarov, V. (1973) *Slovo o perevoda* [*A Word about Translation*], Moscow: Mezhdunarodnye otnosheniya.

Roganova, Z. (1971) *Perevod s russkogo yazyka na nemeckii* [*Russian–German Translation*], Moscow: Vysshaya shkola.

Chapter 6

Equivalence and adequacy

Alexander Shveitser

It is by no means surprising that the concept of equivalence has loomed so large in the discussion of translation for such a long time. Equivalence goes back to the first use of translation in an educational context: as a proficiency check on language learning. Students would be asked – as far back as Roman times – to translate a text written in the language they were learning to demonstrate their understanding of that text. As a result, students had to bend their own language in their translations to make it fit the mold of the language of the original as much as possible.

Small wonder that ever since Roman times translation scholars who were active as translators themselves, like Hieronymus, tried to devise all kinds of ways around this type of equivalence, whereas translation scholars who did not actually translate themselves, like Catford, would cling to some notion of equivalence as the only yardstick by which the activity of translation could be measured at all.

Throughout the history of translation, equivalence has revealed itself both as a phenomenon that can be located on different levels and as a concept eventually so riddled with contradictions that many translation scholars in the West are now suggesting that it should gently be retired and put to pasture in the company of such other fading glories as representational truth. Russian theorists, on the other hand, seem to want to hold on to some notion of equivalence, mainly, one suspects, for pedagogical reasons. Beginning students of translation indeed need to be told that some of the solutions they come up with are "good," and others "bad," at least until they acquire the self-confidence to contextualize their own endeavor beyond the classroom and to establish for themselves what kind of equivalence, if any, they can realistically strive for in a given situation. In this respect, a pedagogically motivated concept of equivalence functions not unlike the ladder Wittgenstein talks about at the end of the *Tractatus*: you use it to climb to where you want to be, and discard it once you are there.

A. L.

The terms equivalence and adequacy have long been current in translation theory, sometimes loaded with different meanings, often treated as synonyms. Komissarov (1980), though, treats "equivalent translation" and "adequate translation" as two distinct but closely related notions. In his opinion the term "adequate translation" is the broader of the two, and it is often used as a synonym for "good translation," a translation that has achieved the required optimal level of interlanguage communication under certain given conditions. Komissarov understands "equivalence" to mean the correspondence of two linguistic units that can be equated with one another.

Katharina Reiss and Hans J. Vermeer (1984) describe the relationship between adequacy and equivalence in a different way. As they see it, the term equivalence embraces relationships not just between separate units but also between whole texts. Equivalence on the level of units does not necessarily imply equivalence on the level of texts, and vice versa. Besides, the equivalence of texts goes beyond their linguistic manifestation into the cultural dimension.

Adequacy, on the other hand, refers to the correspondence of linguistic units in the source text with linguistic units in the target text, and is therefore taken to be the basic parameter of the translation process. The terms "adequacy" and "adequate" are used in connection with translation as a process, while the terms "equivalence" and "equivalent" are used in connection with the relationship between source text and target text which perform similar communicative functions in different cultures. Reiss and Vermeer therefore see equivalence as just one manifestation of adequacy, namely functional adequacy between source and target text.

Let us now discuss these definitions in more detail. In Komissarov's formulation adequacy embraces only the relationships between linguistic units, not between whole texts. It is understood in a much broader sense by Reiss and Vermeer who take it to include the relationships both between separate units and between whole texts. They specifically point out that equivalence of texts by no means presupposes equivalence on the level of units.

Equivalence and adequacy 49

The relationships between linguistic units that are established with a view to their paradigmatic connections in the context of a language system represent an object of study for contrastive linguistics and not for the theory of translation. In translation theory "equivalence" is established between actual linguistic units as segments of given texts, rather than between linguistic units as such. The data supplied by an experiment carried out by Retsker are suggestive in this respect. A text given to a group of test persons contained the following phrase: "Fresh air revived most of the men and the thought of beer at the nearest pub stimulated sluggish pulses." Ninety-three percent of the test persons translated "the thought of beer" not as "mysl' o pive" but as "mysl' o kruzhke piva" [the thought of a glass of beer]. Naturally the correspondence between "beer" and "kruzhok piva" does not represent a correspondence between these units in the systems of the two languages, but rather a correspondence between segments of texts, totally and completely conditioned by the situation (Retsker 1974: 65–70).

Barkhudarov (1984) discusses the problem of the part played by context in establishing relationships of equivalence in his article "Contextual meaning and translation." He is right to point out that the fact that one or more lexical meanings of an item are not registered does not constitute proof that the item in question is contextually bound. It is not always easy to state with any degree of certainty whether a given lexical unit manifests a peculiar "non-dictionary" meaning in a given context, or whether we are faced with a concretization of the usual "dictionary" meaning. We find, for instance, the following phrase in Harper Lee's novel *To Kill a Mockingbird*: "I don't know of any landowner around here who begrudges children any game their father can hit"/"Ja ne znayu u nas v okruge takogo zemlevladel'tsa, kotoryi pozhalel by dlja etih detei zaica." Since the notions "zaiats" [rabbit] and "dich" [game] are in a hypo-heperonymic relationship, we can hardly maintain that the English word "game" appears in this instance in the peculiar contextually bound meaning of "rabbit." Rather, the translators have resorted here to a device familiar in translation theory as "concretization."

On the other hand, in the next example, taken from J. D. Salinger's *The Catcher in the Rye*, we find a semantic shift in young Holden's words "I'm just going through a phase right now." The Russian translation of this sentence reads: "Eto u menja perehodnyi vozrast." Of all the meanings of "phase" listed in the *Bol'shoj anglo–russkij slovar'* [the *Big English–Russian Dictionary*], the meaning "stupen razvitiya" (stage of development) comes closest. In Barkhudarov's opinion, therefore, the English word "phase" is used in the contextual meaning of "age" [vozrast], which is not a meaning listed in the dictionary.

Summing up the interesting data discussed in his article, Barkhudarov concludes that when they function within the structure of a coherent text linguistic units do not just realize their systemic meaning, as fixed in the language; rather they also acquire new meanings and shades of meaning due to the influence of context and the extralinguistic situation. This is precisely what enables participants in communicative acts to describe not just familiar situations but also the endless variety of possible and even imaginary situations.

Speaking of equivalence we should not forget a very important tenet of the theory of translation, namely that the equivalence of texts should take precedence over the equivalence of segments of texts. This becomes abundantly clear in all cases when the sender's communicative purpose does not highlight the text's referential function but another of its functions, such as the metalinguistic or the "poetic" function. For this very reasons puns cannot be translated on the level of equivalence of verbal units. To quote an example taken from Reiss and Vermeer (1984): "Is life worth living? It depends upon the liver." In French this sentence becomes: "La vie, vaut-elle la peine? C'est une question de foi(e)." And in German: "Ist das Leben lebenswert? Das hängt von den Leberswerten ab."

In the French translation equivalence is not preserved on the level of the word. In English the play on words is based on the homonymy of "liver," the organ, and "liver," the person who lives. In French, on the other hand, it is based on the play on the words "foi," faith, and "foie," liver. The German variant is based on the use of peronymy: "lebenswert," worth living, as contrasted with "Leberswert," the condition of the liver.

The notion of equivalence is inextricably bound up with the notion of invariance. Each instance of equivalence presupposes a relationship between text A and text B, or segments thereof, in which a given invariance has been preserved. The most important common invariant feature significant for all levels and types of equivalence is that of the correspondence between the primary sender's intention and the communicative effect of the target text.

This communicative-functional invariant comprises different semiotic levels and functional types of equivalence.

In cases where the relationship of communicative equivalence includes the semantic and the pragmatic level of the text (equivalence on the syntactic level is optional), as well as all the relevant functions of the source text and the target text, we can pronounce those two texts fully equivalent. Sometimes the relationship of communicative equivalence embraces just one of the levels of semiosis (the pragmatic level, for instance), while equivalence is either partially or completely absent on all lower semantic levels. In such cases we speak of partial equivalence. We also use that same term when we refer to the lack of some (but not all) types of functional equivalence between texts as a whole, or segments thereof. The translation of poetry into prose, for instance, could be equivalent to the original on the level of the referential function, but not on the level of the artistic or poetic function.

In any case, equivalence is a relationship between a primary and a secondary text (or segments thereof). Full equivalence, embracing both the semantic and pragmatic levels, as well as all relevant types of functional equivalence, appears to be an idealized construct. This does not mean that full equivalence does not exist in reality at all. Cases of full equivalence are possible, but as a rule they are encountered under relatively simple communicative conditions in texts with a relatively narrow range of functional characteristics. The more complicated and controversial the demands of a translation (or its "paradoxes"), the slimmer the possibility of creating a text that would be a mirrored refraction of the original.

Both the category of equivalence and the category of adequacy are used to evaluate. Equivalence is used for the results of translation, the correspondence of a text that results from the process of interlanguage communication with certain parameters of the original. Adequacy, on the other hand, is connected to the conditions of the flow of the act of interlanguage communication itself, with its filters and determinants, with the choice of translational strategy suitable to the given communicative situation. In other words, if equivalence answers the question whether the target text corresponds to the source text, adequacy answers the question whether a given translation, as a process, meets the requirements of given communicative conditions.

There is one more important difference between the notions of equivalence and adequacy. Full equivalence presupposes an exhaustive rendering of the source text's "communicative-functional invariant." In other words, it is the highest possible requirement that can be addressed to the quality of a translation. Adequacy, on the other hand, is a category with a different ontological status. It is rooted in the real practice of translating, and that practice often allows for a less exhaustive rendering of the overall communicative-functional contents of the original. Adequacy allows for the assumption that decisions taken by translators not infrequently involve some kind of compromise, that translations require sacrifices and that translators must often put up with some losses during the translation process if they are to render that which is of primary importance in a text: its functional dominant. Moreover, the very purpose of communication not infrequently undergoes some changes in the process of secondary communication, and this inevitably causes some retreat from the ideal of full equivalence between source and target text.

It follows that the demand for adequacy must be optimal rather than maximal in nature: a translation should meet certain (often somewhat incompatible) requirements and fulfill certain tasks in an optimal way. A translation can therefore be adequate even when the target text is equivalent to the source text on just one of its levels of semiosis or in just one of its functional dimensions. Moreover, it is quite possible to achieve an adequate translation of a given source text when certain segments of it are not equivalent to the corresponding segments of the target text. In the musical *My Fair Lady*, for instance, based on Shaw's *Pygmalion*, Professor Higgins makes Eliza sing the song "The rain in Spain stays mainly in the plain." The purpose of this phonetic drill is to make her pronounce the /ei/ diphthong correctly, and not as the /ai/ standard in her Cockney sociolect. In the Russian text of the same musical Eliza has to pronounce the tongue twister "Karl ukral u Klary korall." If we compare this segment of the original with its translation, they can hardly be judged equivalent. Native speakers of English will perceive Eliza's song as an exercise aimed at improving her pronunciation by ridding it of a phonetic feature associated with a lower class London sociolect. The Russian audience will perceive the goal of the exercise as an attempt to teach Eliza to pronounce difficult sound combinations. An important social and evaluative component of the source text is therefore lost in the Russian translation, but the translator's decision can be judged adequate nevertheless.

I venture to think that we might use the following demand as a criterion: all deviations from equivalence should be motivated by objective necessity, rather than the translator's arbitrary judgment. In the latter case we should speak of free translation. In the example just quoted the translator's decision is motivated by the impossibility of using Russian dialectal speech in the target text. Russian dialect forms would undoubtedly sound ludicrous in Eliza's mouth. In the example, the conflict between the situations depicted in the source and target texts can serve as a basis for the choice of a strategy that infringes equivalence, but assures adequacy for the translation as a whole.

Some pragmatically motivated cuts and additions in translations also fall under the heading "adequate translation in spite of the absence of full equivalence." In other words, a translation that is fully equivalent to the source text does not always meet the requirements of adequacy and, vice versa, an adequately performed translation is not always based on relationships of full equivalence between source and target text.

It can be said that we are drawing on the initial meanings of the notions "equivalent" and "adequate." Fully equipollent texts are fully equivalent; texts that are partially equipollent to each other are partially equivalent. A translation is adequate when the translator's decisions correspond to the communicative conditions to a satisfactory degree.

Sometimes deviations from the strict demands for full equivalence prove to be connected with such cultural determinants of translation as translational norm and literary tradition. This is particularly the case in the translations of the titles of works of art (novels, plays, movies). In this sphere free translation has long been permissible, including even thorough renaming for the purpose of meeting the specific demands of new cultural surroundings. The title of the famous novel by I. Il'f and E. Petrov, *Dvenadcat' stul'ev* [The Twelve Chairs], became *Diamonds to Sit On* in its American translation. The deviation from the demand for equivalence was pragmatically motivated by the desire to make the title more attractive and intriguing, and therefore more suitable to the traditions of the receiving culture.

Sometimes titles are changed out of the desire to clarify an allusion that would otherwise have remained obscure to the readers of the translation. The title of Hemingway's *The Sun Also Rises*, an allusion to Ecclesiastes, was changed to *Fiesta* in both the Russian and the British edition. In other cases it may be impossible to find a phraseological equivalent that matches the expressive value of the original title. The title of the British movie *A Square Peg* (a shortened version of the phraseological unit "A square peg in a round hole") was therefore rendered into Russian as *Mister Pitkin v tylu vraga* [Mr Pitkin in the enemy's rear].

It should be noted that partially equivalent adequate translations occur very frequently in fiction, and especially in poetry, where they sometimes create their own tradition in the interpretation of a foreign language writer. In Rossel's words:

> The birth of the Russian Burns in Marshak's translations turned all our images of the great Scotsman upside down. Burns is very different from the original (which was inevitable anyway, since he was, after all, translated by nobody but Marshak himself), but he undoubtedly lives in our imagination quite separately and independently from the Russian poet Marshak. They are two different literary events.
>
> (1967: 25).

The evolution of literary traditions and the change in translational norms connected with them exert considerable influence on our views concerning adequacy in translation. This evolution makes it necessary to create new translations of the classics, even if their previous translations have long been considered unsurpassed, and unsurpassable.

Kashkin compares two different translations of the same lines from Byron's *Childe Harold*:

> Roll on, thou deep and dark blue ocean, roll!
> Ten thousand fleets sweep over thee in vain;
> Man marks the earth with ruin, his control
> Stops with the shore

(1) Klubis', Klubis', lazurnyi okean!
    Chto dlya tebya probeg lyubogo flota?
    Put ot ruin ot veka lyudyam dan,
    No na zemle, a ty ne znaesh' gneta.

(2) Stremite volny, svoi moguchij beg!
    V prostor lazurnyi tshtetno shlem armadu
    Zemli opustoshitel'–chelovek,
    Na sushe on ne vedaet pregrady.

The first translation was made by G. Shengeli, an advocate of formal strictness who, in Kashkin's words, "was quite satisfied with preserving the contours of the stanza and the number and the positions of the rhymes. He failed to notice that all the most important elements contributing to the richness of the original have been sacrificed in the name of rhyme: the stanza's sense, its rhythm, and its overall structure." Since Shengeli wanted to keep the quantitative fullness of details, he preserved a number of words from the original, overlooking the fact that the result amounts to a mere pile-up of words. He has preserved the word "flot" [fleet], but linked it with the modernized "probeg" [race] for no good reason. He renders Byron's "ruins" literally as "ruiny," but the reader has to intuit the connection between those ruins and the "put' … ot veka lyudyam dan" [road of ages given to the people]. Kashkin concludes that "this is not just a poor translation, but a naturalistic text in its very setting" (1977: 436–7).

In analyzing the second translation, made by V. Levik, Kashkin highlights Levik's realistic approach to the translation of a romantic text: the romantic theme of the sea is rendered with realistic accuracy. "This is not just a good translation," Kashkin concludes:

> but first and foremost a translation that is realistic in its setting. It is an example of how a translator can approach a given text (a romantic text, in this particular case), in two different ways: on the basis of realism, or on the basis of naturalism. It is also an example of how a given text, while remaining what we call a 'translation,' changes according to the approach and the methods chosen by its translators
>
> (1977: 438).

Even more prominent modifications in the relationship between source and target texts occur when a translator sets out to translate with a specific purpose related to the translation's intended function, as well as some particular characteristics of the reading audience. An example of this type of translation would be the "philological" translation of *Othello* in prose, made by M. Morozov for actors and the director (cf. Shveitser 1988: 61–2).

All such modifications cannot but influence the relationship of equivalence between source and target text, for the obvious reason that the notion of equivalence is always connected with the recreation of the source text's communicative effect as determined by the initial communicative situation and its components (the initial sender's communicative purpose aimed at the initial audience). Adequacy, on the other hand, as I have already pointed out, is used for the correspondence of a translation to primarily those factors that modify its result and that are introduced by the secondary communicative situation (the translation is directed at a different addressee, in another culture which not infrequently has different translational norms and a different literary tradition, and the translation is often made with a specific communicative goal in mind). It follows that adequacy is a relative notion. A translation judged adequate by one school of translation may be judged inadequate by another.

WORKS CITED

Barkhudarov, L. (1984) "Kontekstual'noe znachenie i perevod" [Contextual meaning and translation], *Sbornik nauchnyh trudov Moskovskogo gosudarstvennogo pedagogicheskogo instituta inostrannyh jazykov imeni M. Toreza* [*A Collection of Working Papers of the Maurice Thorez Moscow State Pedagogical Foreign Languages Institute*], 238.

Kashkin, I. (1977) *Dlja chitatelya-sovremennika: Stat'i i issledovaniya* [*For the Contemporary Reader: Articles and Research Papers*], Moscow: Sovetskij pisatel'.

Komissarov, V. (1980) *Lingvistika perevoda* [*The Linguistics of Translation*], Moscow: Mezhdunarodnye otnosheniya.

Reiss, K. and Vermeer, H. J. (1984) *Grundlegung einer Allgumeinen Translationstheorie* [*The Foundation of a General Theory of Translation*], Tübingen: Niemeyer.

Retsker, J. (1974) *Teoriya perevoda i perevodcheskaya praktika* [*The Theory of Translation and the Practice of Translating*], Moscow: Mezhdunarodnye otnosheniya.

Rossel, V. (1967) "Zaboty perevodchika klassiki" [Problems of the translator of the classics], *Tetrady perevodchika* [*Translator's Notebooks*] 4: 23–34.

Shveitser, A. (1988) *Teoriya perevoda: Status, problemy, aspekty* [*Translation Theory: Status, Problems, Aspects*], Moscow: Nauka.

Chapter 7

A note on phrasemic calquing

Andrei Danchev

"Phraseme" is a term often found in essays written within the Russian and Bulgarian tradition portrayed here, and rarely, if ever, in essays written within the tradition of translation studies as it has developed in the West.

Russian and Bulgarian translation scholars may well have focused on the phrase as a putative "unit" of translation while their colleagues in the West were still fixated on the word. Moreover, since the Russian and Bulgarian tradition of both translating and thinking about translation is younger than that of the West, it went through the analog of the West European renaissance in which translation was supposed to enrich the native language and culture by actively importing foreign words and phrases at a later historical date, which may account for the fact that the memory of this aspect of translation is more alive still within the Russian and Bulgarian cultural and linguistic context.

Russian and Bulgarian scholars also point out that many phrasemes in most European languages can be subsumed under a common stock of Greek and Latin origin, or are not infrequently derived from the Bible, so that there exists a kinship between European languages that has little to do with etymological derivation, as that kinship is nearly always described and explained in the West, but much to do with interactions on the personal, group, and national level. Phrasemes traveled with merchants and missionaries, as well as in books.

The fact that they have been relatively little noticed by translation scholars in the West is an illustration of another paradox of translation: the phraseme may well represent the only level on which translation can be truly transparent after all, since one phraseme can be easily, mechanically substituted for another, at least on the surface level. The ripplings and reverberations caused by such substitutions in the connotational fields linked to either the phraseme as a whole or the individual words it encompasses may pose problems of their own, or enrich languages in ways not necessarily anticipated by either author or translator.

A. L.

Translators are usually expected to achieve the same informational and emotive effect as that achieved by the authors of their source texts. This premise appears reasonable enough and can therefore be said to be universally acceptable. Yet its implementation can, and often does, create problems of one kind or another, as is well known. Opinions may, for instance, differ widely on the subject of the amount and the type of phrasemic innovations that translators are allowed to indulge (themselves) in.

Two inherently conflicting attitudes are evidently in competition here. One requires translators to conform to the norms of what is considered to be standard in the target language, and so to keep that language "pure," whatever that may mean to whatever variety of people. On the other hand, translators have often been known to adopt elements and structures of the source language, enriching the target language as they did so. It is common knowledge that practically all the standard languages of Europe have developed under a strong influence exerted by translations, even if we only think of Bible translations in this respect. This state of affairs has naturally caused not only extensive borrowing of individual lexemes, but also the calquing of entire collocations and set phrases of various types. In what follows I shall consider the latter kind of borrowing.

Interlingual influence is usually strongest on the levels of vocabulary and syntax. It is advisable to recognize the existence of both the conscious and the unconscious transfer of foreign patterns in the course of language contact. Both types of interlingual influence are particularly conspicuous in the area of phraseology.

When is the literal translation of an idiomatic phrase to be qualified as a useful acquisition for the target language, and when does it turn out to be a mere professional blunder? Translators may be acclaimed for enriching the target language but they may also be accused of polluting it with alien elements, so to speak. No rough and ready answers to these questions exist and in most cases translators will have to rely on their own judgment and ingenuity.

Hardly anyone would object today to the use in Bulgarian of phrases originally foreign. "Burya v chasha voda," the Bulgarian equivalent of a "storm in a teacup," which also occurs in Russian, German, Swedish, and some other languages, and which was first taken from French (Solodukho 1982: 136), is one example. Another is "zhrebiyat e xvarlen" [the die is cast], known to have come from Latin. A fair number of popular phrases of biblical origin must be included here, such as "to wash one's hands of something," that have become part of something like an international common stock of phraseology. Originating in one language or another and then spreading to a number of further languages, such phrases have evidently contributed to the emergence of what has been referred to as a "European language league."

While nobody would frown today on the use of set phrases such as the ones mentioned above, the acceptability of some more recent instances of phrasemic calquing in some recent Bulgarian translations from English is much less assured. This happens when the meaning of the components of a given phrasemic calque is not sufficiently transparent and so contravenes the usual practice of calquing.

In both fictional and other texts recently published in Bulgaria, for instance, readers may come across Bulgarian calques of English set phrases such as "to let the cat out of the bag," "to flash a smile," "to cough up money," "to grow up" (in the figurative sense of acquiring experience), "to make a long face," "to compare notes," and many others that would be rendered differently in normal Bulgarian usage.

In certain cases, such as "to throw a spanner in the works," the Bulgarian comes close to an existing phrase whose English translation would be something like "to put a stick in the wheels."

It could be claimed that Bulgarian calques of such phrases are not true phraseological units because they are not widely used – yet. In that case they could be labeled instances of the translator's lack of experience. On the other hand, there is no watertight distinction between norm and usage, and at least some of the examples mentioned above could be considered instances of incipient usage. In short, today's error could be tomorrow's norm.

Most of the examples I have given so far have been taken from texts translated by established professional translators. These texts have been published in more or less prestigious publications. It is difficult to decide in each particular case whether a given calque is caused by professional inexperience and/or negligence, or whether it reflects a deliberate attempt at introducing stylistic novelty into the translation. Such assessments would obviously require additional research. In any case, judging by the spread of some of these phrases it may be tentatively predicted that they will find wider acceptance in present-day Bulgarian usage, especially in the case of phrases with a relatively more transparent semantic motivation, such as "to be on thin ice," "to be in the same boat," "to rock the boat." It is of course difficult to predict which of these phraseological units will become permanently established in Bulgarian, but there is little doubt that some of them will, in the same way in which so many other set phrases translated from other languages have become part of Bulgarian.

The influence of translation can also cause an existing target language phrase to modify its meaning. The colloquial, and even slangy, Bulgarian expression "vrazvam nyakomu tenekiya" [to tie a can to somebody] is listed in the *Phraseological Dictionary of the Bulgarian Language* as meaning "to put to shame, to deride strongly." This meaning corresponds to the meaning that the phrase also has in some neighboring Balkan languages. Yet in today's colloquial Bulgarian the phrase means "to stand somebody up, to go back on a promise," which is precisely the meaning in which it occurs in the works of authors such as Mark Twain and P. G. Wodehouse, who have been translated into Bulgarian.

Another possible source of calques in current Bulgarian may be the speech of some Bulgarian teachers of English, and of bilingual speakers of English and Bulgarian in general. In fact, the picture would be left incomplete if interesting examples of what could be called "phrasemic code switching" were to be left unmentioned. Obvious examples in this category are "to pull one's leg," "it's raining cats and dogs," "to kick the bucket," "to throw a party," "to take/have a nightcap," "help yourself," "once in a blue moon," "to be in somebody's shoes." Such occasional calques are used consciously by people who work with English professionally as translators, interpreters, and/or teachers. The latter may not infrequently imitate and ridicule their students (though not in their presence, and I would not presume the appropriateness of such conduct) who often translate such phrasemes literally into their native language without being aware of the fact that this practice may constitute an "error" on their part. In other words, teachers consciously exploit what learners do unconsciously, especially when the resulting calque turns out to be vividly expressive and does not hamper communication. On the other hand, learner translations of phrases like "to bear in mind," in which the English verb is erroneously interpreted as referring to birth, thereby distorting the whole phrase into something like "to be born in thinking," are not suitable for communicative purposes.

It may be claimed that some of these calques, especially the ones resulting from fully conscious and deliberate literal translation, tend to sound like holophrastic chunks of the foreign language and can therefore be described as a specific type of code switching. In the case of individual lexemes code switching has actually been described as a stylistic device used for affective reasons such as humor, irony, and denigration (Baetens Beardsmore 1986: 57), precisely the same factors that often determine the deliberate use of such calques in Bulgarian. Indeed, what Baetens Beardsmore goes on to say about foreign words fully covers the specific case of code switching involving set phrases as reported here. This type of code switching is not mentioned by Gumpertz (1982: 75–82), who highlights six main functions of conversational code switching. Haugen (1986) only refers to it indirectly. It resorts under a much neglected general additional function of language in the study of linguistics, namely that language also exists for fun and games.

The examples mentioned and discussed here form a continuum. One of the poles is constituted by fully deliberate calquing, the other by unconscious calquing. In terms of Baetens Beardsmore's typology the former can be considered code switching (with certain qualifications), while the latter can be considered interference (or "transfer," in more up to date linguistic parlance). In a number of cases, especially those situated towards the center of the continuum, there is obviously no distinct cut-off point between the two main types.

The examples discussed in this paper confirm the observation made by various authors, among them Soloduxo, that phraseology is easily borrowed, evidently precisely because of its expressive nature. They also lend further support to the claim that translation – and calquing is a kind of translation – may often be a major factor in language change. In this particular case phrasemic calquing is stimulated by specific sociolinguistic factors. The main factor is of course the considerably heightened prestige of English in Bulgaria after the 1989 political events and the concomitant weakening of purist attitudes. Under these circumstances the deliberate adoption and use of phrasemic calques from English often functions as a marker of sociolinguistic prestige and group cohesion for people with a knowledge of English. This process can therefore be expected to continue.

It is quite clear, in conclusion, that the borrowing of foreign phraseology may sometimes be difficult to appraise from a normative point of view. Whenever an unfamiliar phraseme appears in a translation, readers cannot always be sure whether to treat it as a slip of the word processor, not to mention a mistranslation, or as a potentially productive innovation.

WORKS CITED

Baetens Beardsmore, H. (1986) *Bilingualism: Basic Principles*, vol. 1, Clevedon: Multilingual Matters.

Gumpertz, J. J. (1982) *Discourse Strategies*, Cambridge: Cambridge University Press.

Haugen, E. (1986) "Bilinguals have more fun!," *Journal of English Linguistics* 19: 106–20.

Nicheva, K., Spasova-Mihailova, S., and Cholakova, K. (1974–5) *Frazeologichen rechnik na balgarskiya ezik* [*Phraseological Dictionary of the Bulgarian Language*], Sofia: Bulgarian Academy of Sciences.

Solodukho, E. M. (1982) *Problemy internacionalizacii frazeologii* [*Problems of the Internationalization of Phraseology*], Kazan: Kazan University Press.

Chapter 8

Norms in translation

Vilen Komissarov

There are two main reasons for the long and virtually unchallenged reign of the normative approach in most thinking about translation since the Romans. The first is the use of translation in the context of language learning, as evoked above. The second and more important reason is the historical coincidence that the foundation text of the main religion of the West, the Bible, proved accessible to the great majority of the faithful, clergy and laity alike, only as a translation. This accident of history has tied translation and power together, in a union sometimes unholy and perceived as indissoluble for centuries. The progressive secularization of Europe did little to reverse the normative approach which came to rest on the institutionalized power of critics, philologists, and linguists. Only in the last three decades has the reign of the normative begun to crumble rapidly. It is now generally accepted that no general norms can be given for all translational activity, a realization linked to the realization that translation is an activity *sui generis* after all. As long as translation was considered mainly a secondary activity to be left to robot-like figures, there was little point in admitting that instructions might sometimes have to be diversified. After all, why confuse the machines?

Present-day translation studies tend to analyze norms, not prescribe them, and the analysis appears to reveal the contiguous existence of two types of norms: those established as a function of the type of text to be translated (sonnets or computer manuals) and those established as a function of the type of translation to be made, since in certain situations, and for certain target audiences, a translation of type A (more paraphrastic, say) may be more conducive to successful communication of the original than a translation of another type. Once again, translators are treated as living human beings who have to establish the norms best suited to a particular text in a particular situation, guided by both their experience and their expertise.

A. L.

The notion of a "norm for translation" has not yet been defined strictly enough in contemporary linguistics, even though its theoretical and practical importance are beyond any doubt. Moreover, there is also no general consensus on the parameter of problems that constitute the object of a study such as the present one.

The problem of norm(s) is usually discussed in connection with matters concerning the practical applications of translation theory. To what extent, it is asked, should this theory be normative, to what extent should it strive to formulate some principles, rules, and recommendations? The underlying expectation is, of course, that observation of these principles, rules, and recommendations will guarantee that actual translations will be of a higher quality than they have been until now. Principles, rules, and recommendations are also expected to lead to a certain *réglementation* of the translation process, and to the formulation of a number of criteria for evaluating its results. Translations that meet these criteria will be judged "good," and translations that fail to meet them will be judged "bad," of course.

The authors of earlier works on linguistic translation theory were convinced that it was the task of such a theory to

> serve as a theoretical basis for the practice of translation, which could guide it in the search for the necessary means of expression, and enable it to choose between them. It would also supply them with arguments and proofs in favor of a given decision on a certain concrete problem.
>
> (Fedorov 1953: 12)

It is only natural that such an approach should call for primary concentration on the normative aspect, and inquire what demands translators *should* meet, and how. The theory of translation was thought to be a purely applied discipline, arriving at generalizations on the basis of the creative activities of the best translators. The applied nature of the linguistic theory of translation has also been stressed in many later works. This is the reason why many linguistic studies of translation are constructed on a recurring pattern, starting with a definition of a "correct" translation, and going on to discuss the ways, means, and methods of "achieving adequacy." All such studies are undoubtedly normative in character in as far as the very definition of an "adequate" or "equivalent" translation (as opposed to that of "translation" in general) contains a qualitative element and therefore establishes a certain norm for translation.

The normative approach to translation has repeatedly been the object of criticism from various points of view, mainly for the extreme inconsistency and incompatibility of its recommendations. Many of the principles of translation, formulated as demands that translators should meet, turned out in fact to be mutually exclusive. Translators were admonished to "exhaustively render the content of the original," while being urged, at the same time, to sacrifice certain parts of it for the sake of other, more important parts. They had to translate "thoughts," rather than "words," while at the same time "taking great care to render even the most exquisite nuances" in the meanings of the words. The list is endless.

A normative approach to the process of translation presupposes first and foremost a definition of a norm for translation. So far such a definition is lacking, even though the terms "literal" and "free" translation have been borrowed from the study of literary translation to characterize different deviations from such a norm, and are now widely used in translation studies in general. Clearly those terms can only be tentative. The term "literal translation" usually carries a negative implication. It is used to refer to instances in which translators deviate from the lexical, grammatical, stylistic, and generic norms of the target language because of the interference on the part of the corresponding norms of the source language. "Free translation," on the other hand, obviously does not deviate from any target language norms, but it fails to achieve a sufficient degree of equivalence to the source text. The term "free" is also used as a positive characteristic for a translation that "satisfies the necessary conditions" (Catford 1967: 25–6).

The evaluative terms "adequacy" and "equivalence," often used to denote "correct" translations within the normative approach, have also escaped strict definition. They have been described in ways too vague and general and cannot therefore be applied to the evaluation of concrete translations. Two favorite descriptions appear to be "a recreation of the unity of the original's form and content by means of a different language" (Retsker 1950: 159), and an "exhaustive rendering of both the form and the notional content of the original in a functionally and stylistically adequate manner" (Fedorov 1968: 151). Both formulations presuppose that it is possible to compare "the unity of form and content" of a text, or to "exhaustively" describe its content. They also use terms like "recreation" and "exhaustive rendering" in an unreflected, conventional way. Small wonder, then, that the degree of adequacy exhibited by various translations is often judged differently by different authors. Revzin and Rozentsveig (1964), for instance, consider it wrong to translate the word "bonhomme" in the first paragraph of Daudet's *Un teneur de livre* as "nekij starichok" [some old man], while Fedorov quotes the same translation as an example of accuracy (1953: 134).

Barkhudarov suggests that the definitions of adequate, literal, and free translation be grounded in the classification of translation units on different levels (1969: 9). In that case the quality of translation would be determined by the correct choice of level of translation units.

An adequate translation would be a translation made on a level necessary and sufficient to render the content of the source text unchanged while observing the norms of the target language.

A literal translation would be a translation made on a level lower than necessary for rendering the content of the source text unchanged while observing the norms of the target language.

A free translation would be a translation made on a level higher than necessary and sufficient for rendering the content of the source text unchanged while observing the norms of the target language (Barkhudarov 1969: 9–12).

Barkhudarov points out that a literal translation is, by definition, totally inadmissible, while a free translation tends, on the whole, to be more acceptable. He goes on to soften this rigid formulation somewhat by adding that this judgment depends on the generic features of the source text.

> If free translation is quite admissible and often encountered in the translation of literature, it is completely out of place in the translation of legal or official diplomatic texts. In those cases a literal translation is to be preferred to a free one.
>
> (Barkhudarov 1969: 12)

These definitions give a much clearer picture of the notion under discussion but they cannot easily be applied to the evaluation of actual translations. The separation of translation units on different levels as the result of a comparative analysis does not yet mean that these levels really exist in the process of translation. The choice of level can, on the contrary, be quite irrelevant to the quality of the translation.

The sentence "The people were not slow in learning the truth," for instance, can be adequately translated both on the word level and on the phrase level. "Lyudi ne zamedlili unznat' pravdu" is just as acceptable as "Lyudi bystro uznali pravdu." The translation of "he is a regular ass," quoted in Barkhudarov as "on regulyarnyi osel," is, on the other hand, unacceptable since it violates the combinatorial lexical norms of the Russian language. It should be judged "literal" on Barkhudarov's own terms, because it is made on the word level, not the phrase level. But the choice of level does not influence the quality of the translation in this case either, since this same sentence could perfectly well be translated on the word level as "on prosto osel."

It is particularly difficult to judge whether the correct choice of translation unit has been made on the levels of the sentence and the text. Is the choice of level in the translation of the following stanza of Béranger's, for instance, correct or not? The original reads:

> Il est un petit homme
> Tout habillé de gris
> Dans Paris

B. Kurochkin's translation has:

> Kak yablocko rumyan
> Odet ves'ma bespechno
> Ne to, chtoby ochen' p'an
> A vesel beskonechno

This question can obviously only be answered by the very existence of another variant translation, endowed with the same artistic merits but corresponding to the original on a lower level than Kurochkin's.

Some literary translators regarded the attempt to establish normative principles and approaches as a threat to their creative freedom. Protest against these attempts therefore often took the form of a total rejection of the very possibility and necessity of a theoretical analysis of translation, referred to exclusively as an art and therefore fundamentally non-linguistic in nature. Because they thought of translation theory as a purely applied discipline designed to formulate practical recommendations, its adversaries kept stressing that any attempted *réglementation* of the translator's activities had to be utterly pointless and even potentially pernicious.

In the face of such criticism some translation theorists resorted to "total defense" and began to claim not only that their concepts were not in the least normative, but also that "normative principles and rules of translation can only be established within certain limits, meaning in comparatively simple cases, and only in a relatively general form" (Fedorov 1968: 26).

Such stipulations did little to clarify the core of the problem. No matter what subjective opinion its author may hold, any concept that formulates certain principles that translators *should* follow, lists certain demands they *have to* meet, and proceeds to judge translations on the basis of those principles and demands, is and remains fundamentally normative.

The normative assumption can, of course, be made concrete to different degrees, and it can be claimed to be valid only in the case of certain definite translations, or types of translation, or even of translation in general. Principles can be formulated as sovereign rules, they can be accompanied by specifications of the conditions governing their application, or they can be hedged with warning about their likely irrelevance (the so-called "exceptions" claimed to be necessary for the existence of any "rule"). The very possibility of formulating a rule general enough to cover all, or almost all, variations of the object of study depends on the level of their homogeneity, and remains an unattainable ideal in most cases. If, on the other hand, "relatively general rules" are formulated, they should at least be applicable in practice. If a "rule" is found to be so general as to allow for different interpretations and to lead to different results, it loses not only its normative character but its expediency as well. A theory that consists of such "rules" cannot claim to be applicable to practice, simply because it has nothing to apply.

The inconsistency and lack of concreteness displayed by certain rules and principles formulated in some studies of translation does not invalidate the normative approach to translation as such. Authors who point out the empirical nature of the normative concept of translation claim that a science attempting to describe translation as a process should be theoretical rather than normative in nature (Revzin and Rozentsveig 1964: 21). They are right to note that since linguistics aims to describe language as it functions in reality and not to prescribe how it should function, a linguistic theory of translation should also describe what we have in reality, rather than what we should have. On the other hand, linguistics not only establishes norms guiding the use of linguistic units; it also codifies them, thereby introducing such notions as "literary norm" and "correct linguistic usage."

What I have said so far shows that we do not have sufficient grounds to consider the linguistic study of translation as a purely applied science and to regard the introduction of translation theory into this branch of applied linguistics as a "contradictio in adiectio," as Karl Bausch does (1971: 55). The basic task of translation studies as a branch of linguistics is the theoretical study and description of the phenomenon of interlanguage communication that people engage in with the purpose of establishing the system of relationships that languages enter into in the process of their mutual co-functioning. This is a task directly related to a number of problems studied in general linguistics. At the same time a linguistic study of translation cannot but try to find an outlet in practice, formulating normative recommendations that could be used by translators as "instructions for action," and that could supply criteria for evaluating the quality of a translation. What I object to is not the attempt to formulate rules for translation, but rather the attempt to do so without a sufficient theoretical basis and at a time when the very notion of norms in translation is still not sufficiently defined. The problem of the norm itself is far from simple and calls for theoretical analysis on many levels. Any attempted solution of the problem ought not to be prefaced by normative instructions of the "the translator should" type. Rather, norm(s) should first be established and described, and only then prescribed, in exactly the same way as usage and norm are first described in a language and then prescribed. Only after norm(s) in translation have been exhaustively described and after all due attention has been paid to modifications likely to occur in different types and under different conditions of translation can we try to formulate rules sufficiently defined to allow translators to follow them in order to achieve desired results. It should be admitted that translation theory, though an "applied" discipline by its very nature, has not become normative so far.

What, then, are the components of the notion "norm" in translation? Linguistics cautions us against any attempt to formulate a norm for translation in the shape of a single rule to be followed in all types of interlingual communication. Rather, the norm should embody several types of normative assumptions that will turn out to be optional or obligatory depending on the function and the nature of concrete acts of translation.

The results of the translation process are evaluated on the basis of correspondence on the levels of content and style between the original and its translation, and also on the basis of the pragmatic function of the concrete act of translation. All these factors are immediately normative in character and they determine both the translator's strategy and the criteria used in the evaluation of the resulting translation. The notion of a norm for translation should also include the requirement that translators should adhere to the norms of the target language and that the result of the translation process should correspond to the generally accepted views on the function and goals of translation that guide individual translators in any given historical period.

The norm for translation could therefore be described as the interaction of at least five types of normative requirements, namely (i) equivalence, (ii) genre and style, (iii) linguistic usage, (iv) pragmatic function, and (v) convention. A detailed description of any of these variants of the norm and their relative importance in guaranteeing a correct translation would fall beyond the boundaries of the present paper. In what follows I shall therefore merely touch on some aspects of the formulation given above.

First of all, it appears of primary importance to distinguish between the terms "adequate" and "equivalent" translation. The first term has a broader meaning and it is used as a synonym for a "good" translation, a translation that meets the demands of interlanguage communication in concrete conditions. The second term, equivalence, has been used in this paper in its purely linguistic sense, namely: "identity of meaning of comparable linguistic units." Equivalence is at the root of communicative identity, the presence of which turns a text into a translation. Adequate translation is by definition equivalent translation, although the degree of identity of meaning between original and translation may differ. The fullest equivalence on the level of linguistic units implies the closest possible correspondence between the content of the texts in the two languages. The opposite is obviously not always true: equivalent translations will not always be adequate translations, since they might display close correspondence between the content of the texts in the two languages while violating some other element subsumed under the norm formulated above.

Equivalence implies the rendering in the translation of the content of the original, that is, the totality of all the information contained in that original, including the emotive, stylistic, aesthetic, and all other functions of the linguistic units. Equivalence is therefore broader than "strict" translation, since that usually implies little more than the preservation of the original's "objective and logical content" as a reference to an identical situation. Equivalence as a norm therefore implies maximal orientation towards the original.

The norm for equivalence in translation is not an invariable parameter. It calls for the highest possible correspondence between the contents of original and translation, but only within the limits compatible with the other normative requirements that guarantee a translation's adequacy. In every specific case the type of equivalence is determined by the co-relation between source and target language units *and* by pragmatic factors that influence the act of translation. Violation of the norm of equivalence can be absolute when a translation is judged non-equivalent, when it fails to render the content of the original on the lowest level, that of the first type of equivalence. A translation may also be judged non-equivalent when it has been established that the other norms for translation could have been met on a level higher than the one actually achieved in the translation. In the first case the translation should also be considered inadequate; it may be considered adequate in the second case, provided maximum correspondence on the content level is not obligatory for the successful achievement of interlanguage communication.

Generic and stylistic norms play an important part in the production of adequate translations, as they define both the necessary level of equivalence and the dominant function of the source text – the two criteria that guide both translators' choices of strategy and actual evaluations of their work. The norm for correct linguistic usage can be established only by taking the stylistic and sociolinguistic differentiations of linguistic usage into account. In the same way normative requirements for an adequate translation are relevant only for certain types of text and certain conditions governing the activity of translation. It would therefore be wrong indeed to use identical criteria for the evaluation of cheap novels and literary masterpieces, patents and musical librettos.

Translation criticism is, in practice, mainly based on an intuitive idea of the generic and stylistic norm. Literary translation is judged by its artistic merit, technical translation by the correct use of terminology that allows the reader to understand the descriptions it contains and to use the text of the translation for practical technical purposes, whereas the translation of advertisements is judged by its effectiveness.

The generic and stylistic norms of translation can therefore be defined as requirements for the translation to correspond to both the dominant function and the stylistic peculiarities of the text type to which the original belongs. The choice of text type depends on the specificity of the original, while the stylistic requirement is to be met by adherence to the normative rules characterizing texts of a similar type in the target language. If a translated text turns out to be a technical description, this presupposes that the original was also a technical description and that the language and style of the translation meet the requirements valid for the production of technical descriptions in the target language. The generic and stylistic translation norms are therefore seen to possess a double orientation, with the proviso that the orientation toward the target text remains dominant.

The problem of the norms regulating the use of translated linguistic usage in the target language has not been studied at all. The language of translation cannot but have certain definite peculiarities originating in the specific nature of this type of linguistic usage activity, as I have pointed out elsewhere (Komissarov 1973: 166). The contact between two languages in the process of translation inevitably leads to the more widespread use of analogical forms and to a degree of relative similarity in the use of linguistic units.

The translated text functions as a product of linguistic usage in the target language, which means that the rules established by target language norm and usage apply to it. Norms and usage vary not only on the level of different functional styles but also on that of accepted literary language. Distinctions tend to be made between colloquial speech, being the language of informal communication, and literary language. Some linguists are inclined to think that the language of science constitutes another specific variant. The secondary nature of translated texts and their orientation toward a foreign language original distinguish them from all other linguistic usage products in their own language. Translated texts in any given language are probably composed in a peculiar variant of language use that cuts across both a language's functional styles and its other variants. The translated text's orientation toward the original inevitably modifies the character of the language units used by translators and tends to bring about their "loosening." A fair number of words, phrases, and ways of describing certain situations are initially found only in the language of translation and they are only gradually absorbed into the target language.

The norm for linguistic usage in translation can therefore be defined as the requirement to follow the rules of norm and usage in the target language in the peculiar variant usage common for translated texts in that language. This variant usage has not yet been described and translators tend to adhere to it intuitively.

The pragmatic setting governing any given translational activity is not a "norm" in the strict sense of the word since the pragmatic superfunction of any translational act may well turn out to be restricted to an individual case and therefore can not be said to be typical for translation as a whole. Yet the modification of the end product of translational activity to suit some pragmatic purpose is a common enough event and any attempt to propose a normative evaluation of translation needs to take it into account. The attempt to carry out a specific pragmatic task represents a kind of superfunction that prevails over all subordinate aspects of the norm for translation. In order to carry out such a task satisfactorily translators may well refrain from any attempt at achieving maximum possible equivalence; they may translate the original only in part; they may change the generic nature of a text and be satisfied with reproducing just some of its formal peculiarities in translation, which will inevitably lead them to break some target language rules of norm and usage. The pragmatic conditions governing the act of translation may also call for the total or partial rejection of translation norms as such, and for the replacement of translation "proper" by rewriting, meaning any kind of rendering of the contents of the original that does not claim to be that original's exhaustive representation.

We should, finally, also take into account that a language community can in any given stage of its history have strictly defined views on the goal and function of translation and on the "right" way to translate. It is well known that different periods in the history of translation have been dominated by different demands. At one time translations had to be literal; at another time they had to improve on their originals; at yet another time they had to be free renderings of originals that were considered untranslatable anyway.

Early translations of religious texts reflected the awe with which translators approached not just the content, but also the letter of their originals. Even now some Bible translators consider a certain degree of incomprehensibility acceptable in view of its effect on the believer. Eighteenth-century French translators considered it their duty to reshape and restructure their originals; if they had failed to do so their translations would not have been acceptable to their readers and critics. In other words the norm established for translation in various historical periods often consisted of violations of various aspects of the norm for translation. It is clear that normative requirements for translation have historically always been formulated on the basis of the reigning "conventional" norm.

The present conventional norm for translation can be described as the requirement for maximum correspondence between translation and original, establishing the translation's ability to function as a full-scale substitute for the original, both in detail and as a whole. In practice this requirement is met by adherence to all or most aspects of the norm for translation defined above.

On the practical level the different aspects of the norm for translation tend to exist in a hierarchical relationship to each other. Both translators and readers of translations focus their attention first on the translation's pragmatic value, on the solution proposed to the problem of the pragmatic superfunction raised in the course of the particular act of translation. The degree to which attention is focused on the norms of translated linguistic usage is determined by the generic and stylistic norms for translation which constitute the second important parameter for the normative evaluation of a translation. The norm of equivalence constitutes the final evaluative requirement, which must be met on condition that all the other aspects of the norm for translation have been met as well. The exhaustive rendering of the content of the original is without doubt the main characteristic feature of interlanguage communication and equivalence therefore constitutes the most "inherently translational" normative requirement. It is defined exclusively by linguistic factors and the degree to which it has been met can be established with the utmost objectivity.

On the other hand, the evaluation of translation equivalence calls for a detailed comparison between original and translation, an activity that requires both high qualifications and a considerable investment of time and effort. People who read and accept the work of translators are usually devoid of the former and not willing to invest in the latter. In practice, even a comparatively low level of equivalence can guarantee the possibility for interlanguage communication provided that all other normative conditions (that can often play a more vital role for the communicators in any given instance) have been met. It should also be noted that achieving maximum equivalence is no easy task, and translators therefore often only succeed in achieving partial equivalence, especially if they are pressed for time or working under unsatisfactory conditions. Paradoxically, therefore, the norm of equivalence often proves the least obligatory requirement in practice.

The many-faceted problem of the establishment and description of (a) norm(s) for translation calls for further investigation that should make it possible to work out objective and practical criteria for a qualitative evaluation of translations.

WORKS CITED

Barkhudarov, L. (1969) "Urovni yazykovoi yerarhii i perevod" [The levels of language hierarchy and translation], *Tetradi perevodchika* [*Translator's Notebooks*] 6.

Bausch, K. R. (1971) "Linguistique comparative, linguistique appliquée et traduction," *Meta* 16: 1.

Catford, J. C. (1967) *A Linguistic Theory of Translation*, Oxford: Oxford University Press.

Fedorov, A. V. (1953) *Vvedenie v teoriyu perevoda* [*An Introduction to the Theory of Translation*], Moscow: Izdatel'stvo literatury na inostrannyj yazikah [Foreign Language Publishing House].

——(1968) *Osnovy obshtej teorii perevoda* [*A Basis for a General Theory of Translation*], Moscow: Vysshaya shkola.

Komissarov, V. (1973) *Slovo o perevode* [*A Word about Translation*], Moscow: Mezhdunarodnye otnosheniya.

Retsker, J. (1950) "O zakonomernyh sootvetstviyah pri perevode na rodnoj yazyk" [About regular correspondences in translation into the native tongue], *Teoriya i metodika uchebnogo perevoda* [*The Theory and Practice of Teaching Translation*]. Moscow: Vysshaya shkola.

Revzin, I. and Rozentsveig, B. (1964) *Osnovy obshtego i mashinnogo perevoda* [*The Basis of General and Machine Translation*], Moscow: Vysshaya shkola.

Chapter 9

Comprehension, style, translation, and their interaction

Margarita Brandes

Comprehension precedes translation, of course, or is at least generally supposed to do so. But comprehension is by no means limited to translation: the problem of comprehension arises at least to the same extent with an original as with a translation. Many, not to say most, studies of translation in the West resolutely sidestep the problem of comprehension mainly by stating that it belongs to the realm of either epistemology or anthropology and that the translation scholar is not qualified in either.

This results in the somewhat strange situation that the very foundation of translational activity is not deemed to belong within the realm of competence of the translation scholar, or at least that it is generally accepted that translation scholars should accept the findings of philosophers and/or anthropologists. Never is the suggestion made that translators and translation scholars may have something meaningful to contribute to the debate on comprehension, precisely because this potentially meaningful contribution is based on their own experience, direct or indirect, of the activity of translation. Russian and Bulgarian translation scholars do not share the reserve of their Western colleagues in this respect. Essays like the following are by no means as rare as one could expect, and they are written from the conviction that the field of translation need not be passive, receptive only, but that, as a full-fledged field of enquiry in its own right, it is entitled, even obligated, to contribute to interdisciplinary discussions on the basis of its own practice and research.

A. L.

This paper proposes some observations on the object of translation and its goal, based on a stylistic approach rooted in the understanding of communication as an ongoing activity. The situation in translation studies is similar to that in stylistics. This is not a coincidence, since translation and stylistics have their common roots in hermeneutics. We can therefore legitimately ask the question whether stylistics and translation belong to the category of artistic or of scientific phenomena: are they crafts or do they provide explanations? We have an answer for translation: it is both a craft and a science. Moreover, in the science of translation we have already reached the level of interpretation, which may guide translation to its own purely theoretical level. Indeed this is a normal evolution, since the development of a science as a whole is inseparable from the constant deepening and concretization, not to mention radical re-evaluation, of the concepts current in it.

In our time a theory is considered to be the logical model of an object of research that has been strictly defined. What criteria allow us to define the object of translation? Many problems arise here. The most basic question appears to be whether translation has to do with substance, in which case it should be regarded as the product of linguistic usage, or with function, in which case it should be regarded as a process, realized by means of signs, or even with action, in which case it should be regarded as a synthesis of substance and function. If the object of translation is an activity, then what kind of activity are we thinking of: primary, secondary, creative, multiplicatory? What should be modeled for the purpose of recreating the object of translation?

Translation seems to be a phantom changing its contours and its inherent properties depending on the positions different scholars occupy. It is therefore necessary first of all to define the very notion of translation and to establish the true parameters of the concrete nature of this object as well as the common hierarchy shared by all its types and forms. In my opinion this hierarchy can be established on three levels of concreteness.

Translation is an activity, both spiritual and practical, related to the activity of communicating. As a result it shares in all the characteristic features of the category of activity in its broadest sense.

Translation is not a productive but a reproductive activity, not a primary but a secondary activity.

This secondary, reproductive activity avails itself of the material offered by natural languages on the basis of the correlation between norm and value. It is therefore a *linguistic-textual* activity.

On the second level of concreteness we shape the specific terms and notions relevant to the peculiarities of the given object. The first level of concreteness is integrative in nature since it includes translation among a group of related activities. The second level of concreteness differentiates the activity of translation and helps to construct a more detailed and exact translation model. Through its connection with bilingual communication the third level of concreteness provides a synthesis of the invariants of the object or objects of translation.

It should be understood that an approach that regards translation as an activity extends also to the result of that activity: the translation as a product, intended for further reception.

The product of a primary spiritual and practical activity, the original text, is reproduced as a system in the product of a secondary activity, the translation. It is true that only separate segments of the original can be used in different pragmatic types of translation, but in such cases the end product is a relatively new entity with a fully independent function of its own, as is the case, for instance, with a summary of a translation of a paper.

Within the wider framework of translation as a secondary activity we can proceed to distinguish (i) a secondary, dependent translational activity, which comes close to multiplication, circulating the original to a wider audience, as is the case with official documents, business documents, scientific and technical data, and (ii) a secondary, relatively independent translational activity resulting in fiction and essayistic texts.

Mutual understanding, the establishing of meaningful contact, is the most basic of the many fundamental characteristics of translation. If the basic category of the primary productive activity is knowledge accompanied by understanding, the basic category of the activity of translation is not just reception, as many approaches to translation claim, but understanding and interpretation accompanied by knowledge.

The translation process, oriented toward the creation of the product of the translating activity, the text of the translation, is a very complicated system consisting of two subsystems.

The first subsystem, "text interpreter," is a modeled process of revealing the organization of the text on the level of sense. It is the primary translation strategy that regulates the translation process in its second stage in which the sense that has been revealed is recoded in the target language. This sense system, or normative–evaluative system, of the source text is a universal text category, independent of the languages in which it materializes.

The second subsystem, "text norm agent," is unique in character in that it is closely connected to the national specificity of a language. It does not realize abstract, functional contents, but figurative, material contents instead. This subsystem works to establish the different kinds of correspondences between the two languages that function in the translation. It represents the third limitation, the third concretization of the object of translation. In this stage the translational activity is creative in nature: its creativity resides in the choice among several options. The translational activity is therefore both predetermined by the deep normative–evaluative subsystem of the original and free as far as the relationship between source and target language is concerned.

The limitations and concretizations pointed out above establish the boundaries of translation, its structure, its nature, and its functions (achieving adequacy of understanding). In so doing they point the way to the solution of the basic problems raised by translation: translatability, adequacy, the combination of creative and non-creative elements in the act of translating, and the inherent inclusion of the problem of linguistic equivalence in the whole system of tasks that translation is supposed to perform.

The definition of the object of translation is further connected with the existence of norms for translation. These norms have a dual nature and they depend on the mechanisms of understanding. Texts are of interest to translation both as products, reflecting the comprehensive and communicative aspect of translation, and as signs or objects meant to be interpreted and understood.

Being normative–evaluative sign systems, the norms for translation serve as the basis for the concrete linguistic decisions that need to made. The decisions themselves belong to the domain of natural language.

The approach to translation theory offered here differs in principle from other approaches. The translational activity is traditionally supposed to be linked with thinking and based on reflection. Traditional approaches also have a lot to say about sense when they discuss content. In contrast, my approach is squarely based on thought-language activity, together with the secondary knowledge about the world acquired in the process of communication that is connected with the activity of communicating information and results in the production of meaningful texts. My approach is therefore not oriented toward the material and factual basis of the text, its ideas, or its semantics. Instead, it is programmatically oriented toward the operational side of the content, the functional content or, in other words, the sense.

I therefore suggest that the object of translation should be the translational norm. That norm operates on two levels: the level of projection, which is universal, and the level of realization, which is unique. I further suggest the category of understanding as a basis for a method for the study of translation. This method consists of a system composed of inner and outer attributes. Among its necessary outer attributes are the object of translation (a formation of words called the original); the intermediary, or mediator, or translator; and the product of the activity of translation (the text in the target language). Among its necessary inner attributes are the comprehension of the structure of the sense of the original, which constitutes the basis for a primary translation strategy, more global in nature, and the creation of a secondary translation strategy, more narrowly focused within the framework of the primary strategy. Both the inner and the outer attributes need to be addressed if the method of understanding is to be applied with any degree of success.

UNDERSTANDING AS THE BASIS OF THE CORRELATION BETWEEN STYLE AND TRANSLATION

Style is the way in which language is used in various socially differentiated situations. As a result, it is the system of language used in a given formation of words, or text, for the purpose of exerting axiological (subjective–evaluative) influence.

On the receptive–communicative level on which we analyze translation as the object of a theory, style is the program for mutual understanding between the author of a text (which represents the actual communication) and its reader.

Normally a text is the finished product of understanding and not the expression of a process of understanding. What we write and talk about while trying to explain something is a far cry from what actually goes on in our head during the process of understanding. If we are to understand a text we have to differentiate between its content and its sense. A text is a unified structure made up of statement and communication. It consists of statements about the real state of affairs (its content), and commands or algorithms for action (its sense). The statements are the semantics of the text, the commands its pragmatics. The pragmatics of a text comes into being as a metalanguage and it is always present in the process of communication. In the approach advocated here the analysis of understanding can only be pragmatic. I shall try to analyze the triad style–understanding–translation from the pragmatic point of view. The growing interest in the pragmatics of language that we are witnessing at present has helped reveal the inner connections between language and the universal structures of man's activity.

The text as a finished product consists of three autonomous but closely interrelated cognitive fields: the content that is the result of the formulation of thoughts (the semantics of the text), the communication of content (the syntax of the text), and the effectiveness of the communication of the content (the pragmatics of the text).

The communication of content as well as the effectiveness of that communication are linked with communication in its fullest sense, namely human intercourse. Style is also connected with interaction since it is a semiotic system, not a material-content system. The element of individual knowledge is important for the study of style in relation to understanding. In this context the socio-cultural aspects are more important than the gnoseological aspects. Intercourse as a semiotic system realizes the process of the formulation of thoughts, the primary operation of thinking that lies at the basis of understanding. In reality intercourse exists as a synthesis of linguistic usage and language as a system. A characteristic feature of this synthesis is that the shaping of linguistic form takes place on the basis of and in accordance with the form of linguistic usage. This presents an intermediate starting point for shaping that exists in the already shaped language of a text as a seemingly non-material part of this synthesis. The activity of understanding is connected with the deciphering of this synthetic form in all its complexity, rather than with the deciphering of the linguistic form only.

It is important for translators to learn how to read a text in its inner form, to learn to discover the author in a text, the creator in a "product," to understand the outer text in its inner dialogical form. To do this, translators have to understand the text within the framework of larger forms of thinking.

It is difficult to formulate a logical method that would allow translators to discover the creator in a text, the inner motion of thinking in its traditional structure. It calls for a second reading of the text that reveals another text inside it, constructed from different materials that lie on the other side of the printed text and reveal the "inner pattern" of its logical movement, its inner form. The first reading is based on the subject–predicate structure of the sentence; in the second reading the text appears as a whole.

But what do we have to trigger in the text as we have it to make it reveal its inner form, and so to make it present itself as a whole?

We have been aware for a long time of the similarity between the operations of producing and understanding a text. It is obvious that the understanding of a text requires not just knowledge of the language in which it is produced, but also a definite set of interrelated data concerning both the content of the text and a knowledge of the invariant communicative structures that constitute its form. It is possible to formulate the following well-grounded hypothesis: the structure and the semantics of a text can be regarded as one component of a complex mechanism, whose matching other component is to be found in the mind and memory of the person receiving the text. When these two matching components begin to interact the process of reception and understanding takes place.

We all know from our own irrefutable experience that understanding exists both as a process and as the final summing up of that process. Understanding as a necessary element of every type of human intercourse is a precondition for adequate reaction. Understanding is expressed not so much in the correlation between the original's denotive content and its translation as in the matching of the programs of production and reproduction.

STYLE AS AN ELEMENT OF THE SECONDARY SOCIAL SUBSYSTEM OF THE TEXT

Style is not linked to understanding on the basis of thinking itself but on the basis of information about thinking. Thinking itself would be something like Hegel's "material thinking," which sticks to the content of the text. Information about thinking, on the other hand, is more like Hegel's "discursive thinking," which is not only "free" from that content, but also displays a rather "arrogant attitude" toward it.

That arrogance is obviously rooted in the fact that social relationships which it reflects and formalizes in the course of its activity constitute the object of discursive thinking. These relationships exist in the text as information about "material thinking" in the form of a layer of non-obvious knowledge: linguistically non-articulated and non-verbal context. They constitute the part of translation studies in which the problem of understanding is most acute. It is through this layer that the wider context of the social totality penetrates into the text, and the activity of generating the verbal product is obviously carried out against the background of that social totality. That same social totality also serves as the basis of the normative–evaluative system. Within the framework of that system is shaped the operational structure of the text, universal with regard to translation and governing both the understanding of the text and its recoding into another language. The system of "discursive thinking" lies at the roots of the generic and stylistic organization of the text and appears as the secondary social subsystem of that text with all ensuing consequences including, first and foremost, the characteristic features of its linguistic usage.

Natural language is unique as a social product. The creation of linguistic products always takes place in the context of social life and that social life is inevitably bound up with certain concrete historical conditions. Linguistic products cannot therefore be unique. Words are not indifferent signs for objects that can easily be replaced by equivalent signs in other languages. Natural language is a system, the only system that is at the same time total and open, allowing for different ways of expressing every possible kind of "content" culled from the unlimited variety of human experience.

What matters in the process of communication, however, is not only the material nature of language and its objective properties, but also communicative adequacy and the possibility of its realization. Unambiguousness of communication and correspondence between the immediate experiences of separate individuals guarantee intersubjectivity. Intersubjectivity in turn presupposes the existence of a universal language that must possess the characteristic feature of expressing structural relations linked with the social context. This universal language, or rather metalanguage, is a formal language. Through it a normative–evaluative system is inserted into the text that plays the part both of a program for understanding and of a norm for the translation of the genre of a text and its style. For the purposes of translation it is important to distinguish between the normative–evaluative systems in which the sense of a text is shaped and the normative–evaluative systems in which it is deciphered.

STYLE AND TRANSLATION

Soviet translation studies have consistently eschewed both the absolutization of objective sources and the exaggeration of the importance of the subjective factor. This does not mean, however, that subjective and objective elements are considered as two subsystems of the translation process in perfect balance and enjoying equal rights. Rather they are inseparable and interrelated, and they influence each other. Nevertheless, the creativity that translators display is secondary and its independence relative. The translational ideal that the greatest masters of translation strove to achieve naturally reflects the leading part played by objective factors in their relationship with subjective sources. The concrete ratio of these relations depends on the individual translations but it is conditioned by the original's parameters in which the author's communicative goal has been objectivized. The objective ratio is therefore fixed in the original text and it emerges as the standard for translation adequacy. Ignoring this objective ratio results in the creation of a gap between original and translation and in the deformation of the most important features of the original's content and functions. The subjective side has its own, more flexible standard.

As the result of a secondary and relatively independent activity, translation is closely tied to the original as a product of primary creativity and plays the part of its variant. Style is connected with the primary activity, translation with the secondary activity. Translation must contain elements of "strict preservation" side by side with creative elements connected with the technique of translating, resulting in a certain comparative independence from the product that is the result of the primary creative act. In a translation we find a certain gravitation toward the culture of the contemporary epoch. Translation as a product presents us with a qualitatively defined, relatively closed entity. Yet at the same time it is an "unbound, open" system characterized by a certain adaptability to current concrete historical conditions.

The relationship between style and translation can be described in terms of the dialectically related categories of symmetry and difference. These are inseparable poles, each of which presupposes the other. No concrete instance of identity is possible without some difference and every concrete instance of difference presupposes a measure of identity.

Translation has two functions: one is reproductive, the other assertive. The reproductive function is connected with decoding: it does away with the coded form of the language of the original. The assertive function is the objectivation of the product of primary activity in another language, the transfer of the original from the sphere of primary, creative activity into that of secondary activity. The statement function embodies translation's function of transformation. It is intricately bound up with understanding as the essence of the translation process.

To understand style as an intermediary in translation it is essential to discover the archetype, the historically established framework within which style is understood. That framework appears as the ideal projected for the original, constructed on the basis of the intersubjective, universal aspect of understanding. The creative aspect of translation expresses itself within the scope of two languages: formalized language and natural language.

STYLE AND TRANSLATION AS SELF-ORGANIZING SYSTEMS

Normative–evaluative systems are essentially self-organizing in that they are characterized by processes governing information. Information as a factor in organization and government is of necessity embodied in its bearer. The concrete bearer of a given item of information is its code. The connection between a given item of information and its concrete bearer in a given self-organizing system (SOS) is called code dependence. Since information exists only in the form of a certain code, access to it is possible only by means of deciphering the code, of understanding the code dependence. Deciphering codes in the broadest sense goes far beyond the framework of cognitive and any other conscious activities. It is a fundamental operation that expresses the purposeful functioning and development of any SOS as a result of code switching.

Understanding involves comprehension of the "sense," "values," and "goals" embodied in a given SOS and its product, the text. Deciphering a code is usually described as decoding. However, since information does not exist apart from its concrete bearer, it cannot exist apart from the concrete code either. Decoding therefore really means transforming an unfamiliar code into a familiar one. The familiar code is the one that is regarded as "natural" for the SOS; the unfamiliar code is regarded as strange to it. The natural code is an element of a given SOS as a historically developed coding organization. Deciphering a code therefore means transforming an unfamiliar code into a natural one. Once it has found a way to carry out this transformation, the SOS assimilates the "unfamiliar" code and that "unfamiliar" code becomes "natural" to it. As a result a new functional subsystem appears within the framework of a given SOS.

Transformation of codes occurs on an intersubjective basis and an SOS is constructed on that same basis. Redundancy resides in the fact that language has a "double lining." It is meant to allow for a second reading of the object of the experience described, parallel to the obvious understanding of it. The sense is here constructed in such a way that it can be called double or triple sense, in that the first, verbal sense points toward a secondary and tertiary sense that exist only in figurative form. Because of this duality, or contextuality, language possesses the ability to grasp and exhaust the object of experience simultaneously on several levels.

Chapter 10

A psychological analysis of translation as a type of speech activity

Irina Zimnyaya

Even though many normative approaches to the phenomenon of translation over the last forty years have reveled in the construction of ever more intricate models making use of all kinds of boxes in all kinds of sizes and shapes, linked by all kinds of arrows in all possible and impossible directions, the mind of the translator has always been the black-box that has not been included, or at least not actively mapped, in these schemes. And why should it have been? Ideally it should merely interiorize the model described, turn itself into the box that contains all the other boxes and their arrows.

Russian and Bulgarian translation scholars have been quicker than their colleagues in the West to acknowledge that translators have a somewhat independent mind after all, and to try to describe what goes on in that mind, a type of research that makes all the more sense if one reflects that mistakes, "glitches," variants, and changes in translations are not the result of a mechanistic application of models, but of the conscious activity of the translator's mind. Maybe the translator does not want to receive the original the way the author wants him or her to. Maybe he or she is not allowed to do so by all kinds of circumstances. Maybe the translator (particularly of older texts) is quite simply unable to conceptualize the original, or at least certain of its features, in the same way as the author of that original did. Maybe there is no logical reason at all for certain choices that translators make during the process of reproduction of the original; maybe they pick this word instead of that, this phrase instead of that simply for such all too human reasons as "it just sounds better." This is the reality of translation, not the model. It is refreshing to see that some translation scholars are actually beginning to study the reality, rather than conveniently subsuming it in the free-floating complexities of models.

A. L.

As is well known, translation presents us with

> a multifaceted object of study. The problems of translation can be discussed from various points of view, historical, cultural, literary, linguistic, and psychological, since the translator's activity presupposes definite processes that take place in the sphere of psychic activities and since it bears on the problem of the psychology of creativity.
>
> (Fedorov 1968: 22)

Lately, translation has also been studied from the point of view of general psychology, philosophy, and anthropology as a type of human activity, and as a particular type of linguistic communication. In spite of the generally accepted linguistic understanding of translation as the substitution of an utterance in one language for an utterance in another, according to certain pre-established correspondence (Revzin and Rozentsveig 1962: 53), no unambiguous psychological definition of this phenomenon has been formulated as yet. Belyaev writes that "linguistic translation should not be considered a particular type of human activity but rather a particular type of thinking process based on speech as such, but not including a specific kind of it" (1963: 162). It is this very thinking process, the "switching of thinking from one language base to another" (1963: 162) that Belyaev considers to be translation. An experimental study of this process, carried out by Benediktov, allowed that scholar to conclude that "interpretation is not a complex thinking process; at the same time, though, its structure cannot be reduced to the sum total of the corresponding two monolingual abilities" (1974b: 312).

Pegacheva also defines translation as a "peculiar instance of speech activity" (1959: 138). She goes on to point out that the act of translating is accompanied by a number of psychological difficulties that have to be overcome. Chief among those difficulties is the switch from the system of one language to that of another.

In this paper I, too, contend that translation is essentially activity. My aim is to show that translation is a complex, specific, secondary type of speech activity. This statement holds true for all forms of translation, but I shall concentrate on written translation and on simultaneous and consecutive interpretation. Translation is a type of speech activity that can be studied alongside other types, such as listening, speaking, reading, and thinking. The analysis of the process of translation will therefore be carried out along three basic lines. First, I shall prove that translation is indeed an activity. This will allow me to analyze it on the basis of existing analyses of activity in general. Second, I shall assume that translation is speech activity, rather than thinking. Third, I shall analyze the complexity, specificity, and secondary nature of this particular type of speech activity in comparison with other types. Defining translation as a specific type of speech activity allows me to carry out a detailed qualitative analysis of the overall psychological content of this phenomenon. It further allows me to compare this process with other processes of speech activity on the same logical basis and by means of the same methodological apparatus.

In defining the concept "speech activity" I shall start from the underlying concept of "communicative human activity." "Activity," meaning the process of direct active or indirect intentional and conscious interaction between subject and environment, consists of socially communicative, socially productive, and cognitive activity. Activity implies a complex, multi-channel process of interaction between people and mediates their interaction with the environment. The basic form of this interaction, carried out through socially and historically established verbal means (language as a system of units supplemented by the rules for using those units) and realized in the speech activity (speaking, listening, reading, and writing) of the partners in communication, is defined as verbal communication. Speech activity can therefore be regarded as an expression of people's socially communicative activity in the process of communication. As such it is characterized by the presence of an object, a product, results, units, means, and ways of realization. As opposed to a process, an activity is also characterized by a definite structure that consists of the aspects of motivating, inducing, orienting, knowing, and performing.

Leont'iev writes: "every activity an organism engages in is directed at one object or other; non-object directed activity is impossible" (1959: 37) What, then, is the object of speech activity? The object of the productive types of speech activity (speaking and writing) is the very thought of the speaker as a reflection of the different ties and relationships between the objects and events of the real world. The object of the receptive types of speech activity (listening and reading) is the thought of an agent who is not the speaker. The fact that thoughts are not material determines the specific "theoretical," rather than objective and practical, character of all types of speech activities.

If the object of speech activity is thought – and the expression of thought is the aim of all types of speech activity – that thought exists, is formed and realized in language. However, the speaker's thoughts can be formed and formulated in different ways with the help of one and the same vocabulary and grammar. This fact is reflected in the manner of the speech activity. It is precisely the manner of the shaping and formulation of thoughts by means of language that we call speech. This definition is rooted in the ideas of Vygotskij and Rubinstein. Vygotskij holds that "outer speech is the process of transformation of thoughts into words, the materialization and objectivization of thought" (1934: 311). Rubinstein adds: "we formulate thought in speech but we shape it while we formulate it" (1940: 350).

Since it is a manner of forming and formulating thoughts by means of language, speech uses language as an instrument. The manner of shaping and formulating thoughts can obviously undergo significant changes. The first change it can be subject to depends on the speaker's communicative intention or the person to whom the communication is directed. Does the speaker address himself or a listener?

We are faced with an inner manner of shaping and formulating thoughts in the first case, and with an outer manner in the second case. Since it is the manner of shaping and formulating thoughts as a subjective form of reflection of relations in objective reality by means of language as a socially based semiotic system, speech represents an amalgam of the social and the uniquely individual, realized both in the process of shaping, formulating, and expressing one's own thoughts (speaking and writing) and in the process of shaping and formulating somebody else's thoughts (listening and reading).

It is important to consider that speech reflects the essential feature of thinking as a process, as well as its dynamic nature, in inseparable unity with the language that embodies the results of many preceding acts of thinking; yet at the same time language plays the role of instrument in every single act of thinking.

A product is also part of the psychological content of any activity. The product is the element in which an activity is objectivized, embodied, and materialized, the aim of the activity and its motive, as well as its object, means, manner, and conditions. The product of the productive types of speech activity (speaking and writing) is the speech message (the text). The product of the receptive types of speech activity (listening and reading) is the judgment a person makes in the process of understanding the speech message that is being uttered.

An activity is not just characterized by a product, but also by a result. The result of the productive types of speech activity is the listener's or reader's verbal or non-verbal reaction. The result of the receptive types of speech activity is the understanding of the message (the positive result of reception) or its misunderstanding (its negative result).

It should be clear that speech activity, like any other form of human activity, displays all the elements of psychological content associated with an activity. Speech activity is therefore an activity in the full sense of the word.

Genetic predisposition in human society favors those types of speech activity that realize oral verbal communication. These are the types of activity shaped in the ontogenesis as a means of reflecting reality as an amalgam of communication and generalization. Reading and writing are more complicated types of speech activity that can only be acquired as the result of special training since they reflect not only the manner of shaping and formulating thought, but also the manner in which the results of the reflection of reality are given fixed form. These four types of speech activities – speaking, listening, reading, and writing – represent the basic types of interaction between partners in verbal communication.

What is translation in all this? Is it the sum of two types of speech activity or is it a complex and separate (sub)type of speech activity? I intend to prove that it is precisely the latter: a separate, complex, and specific type of human speech activity.

In defining translation as a complex type of speech activity I have in mind the nature of the processing of the message that is received and reproduced. If the processing is receptive, in the case of listening and reading, and productive, in the case of speaking and writing, translation is both a receptive and a (re)productive activity. If the process of conceptual reception constitutes the basis of receptive speech activity and the process of creative thinking constitutes the basis of productive speech activity, translation as a complex receptive–reproductive activity presupposes a unitary process of well-developed reception of content, resultative conceptualization, and reproductive thinking.

The complex nature of translation as a type of speech activity is also revealed by the characteristics of the reflection of reality that appears as a "universal and most ancient regularity" in the evolutionary history of the animal world (Anokhin 1969: 124). In the receptive types of speech activity this regularity is demonstrated in the form of probability prognostication; it appears as a cataphoric synthesis in the productive types of speech activity. It is characteristic for translation and for the different types of interpretation in particular that the probability prognostication of what the translator is going to say is made not only on the basis of linguistic experience and communicative situation, but also on the basis of what the translator could say. Consequently, the very nature of cataphoric synthesis is changed inside the overall mechanism of cataphoric reflection. The complex character of the processing of the material that is received and reproduced is also preconditioned by peculiar features in the operation of memory, but I shall defer the discussion of those features until later.

The different types of translation and interpretation are of course characterized by different levels of complexity, depending on the degree of integration between the receptive and reproductive sides of the process, the level of production and the corresponding level of reproduction, and the degree to which memory, the mnemonic human activity, is involved. Judged on the basis of the degree of integration that is involved, simultaneous interpretation is among the most complex types of translation, followed by consecutive interpretation and written translation. Judged on the basis of the level of production, that is, the level of involvement of the creative element in this type of speech activity, the hierarchy is reversed. The hierarchy is characterized by the growing importance of the part played both by memory, especially operational memory, and by probability prognostication as a basis for cataphoric synthesis in interpretation. Under experimental conditions that included an impeded mechanism of probability prognostication, simultaneous interpreters could not manage to achieve a single full and adequate rendering of any sentence. The interpreter's tempo is slowed down considerably. The time given to pauses is considerably longer than that devoted to talking. Since they are not able to build a hypothesis and verify it during the process of listening, simultaneous interpreters find that they have to listen first and speak afterwards, unable as they are to catch the text that is produced while they are speaking (cf. Zimnyaya and Chernov 1970:

111–14; 1974: 115). The absence of the possibility for probability prognostication impedes the mechanism of cataphoric synthesis, or leads to the formulation of a synthesis based on inadequate hypotheses.

Although the complex nature of translation as a type of speech activity is demonstrated most obviously in the nature of the processing of received and reproduced material, it also (pre)determines the characteristic features of such elements of its psychological content as object, means, manner, product, and result. In the productive types of translation (speaking and writing) the object is the speaker's own thought in its development and expression. In fact, it is the very purpose of those types of speech activity to develop those thoughts and to express them. In the receptive types of speech activity (listening and reading) the object is someone else's thought, recreated by the receiver for yet another person or persons. In this type of speech activity the sense of the received message or utterance appears as the receiver's own communicative content. That content can be formulated in ways that are either more or less strict than those governing the formulation of the communicative content of the source utterance. In Benediktov's words: "interpretation is characterized by preservation of sense and change of content" (1974b: 164).

The complexity and the specificity of the object of translation as a type of speech activity can therefore be found in the fact that somebody else's thought is not only received and shaped, but formulated as well. In the receptive types of speech activity only the inner manner of shaping and formulating is used, both by means of the individual object–scheme code and by means of the language system. In translation, written or oral, the use of the outer manner is inevitable. Moreover, while all other types of speech activity are characterized only by the shaping and formulation of thought, translation also implies its reformulation. Reformulation is an inseparable part of the inner mechanism of translation, characterized by different degrees of consciousness and, more importantly, occurring at different points or moments in the process.

Many problems still remain to be solved in the psychological study of translation. Among them are the problem of the qualitative characteristics of the translation process, of the number of stages comprising it, of the nature of the intermediate stage, and of the moment at which the switch from one language to the other takes place. In his detailed three-stage model of translation Benediktov maintains that the most complicated type of interpretation includes

> reshaping of speech signals on five levels: a transition from reception of outer speech to its verbalization, a transition to inner speech in the source language, a switch from inner speech in the source language to inner speech in the target language, a transition to verbalization in the target language and, finally, a transition to outer speech in the target language.
>
> (1974b: 169)

On the basis of the nature of the different combinations of these levels Benediktov distinguishes between sixteen types of interpretation. However, his scheme fails to provide an answer to the question of localization, that is, the precise point or moment at which the switch from one language to another and the transition from one stage to another takes place.

If we regard translation as a continuous process involving the conceptualization (shaping and formulation) of thoughts perceived, the understanding of the sense of a message, its transformation into communicative content, and the shaping and formulation of the utterance itself, we are able to analyze it as a type of speech activity in all its complex specificity. In Belyaev's words:

> the process of translation can be decomposed into three basic stages: the initial stage, involving understanding of the thoughts expressed in one language; the final stage, involving the expression of those thoughts by means of another language, and the intermediate stage, involving the conceptual rethinking of reality, when a thought in one language is substituted for a thought in another, or when a transition takes place from the use of certain concepts to the use of certain other concepts.
>
> (1963: 166)

Let us note first that all conceptualization comes about by means of an inner way of shaping and formulating thought, that is, by means of inner speech. But two questions remain: what language is used, and to what degree is conceptualization achieved? I shall assume that conceptualization is achieved to the highest degree and that its successive phases can even be accompanied by motions of articulation – oral or verbal articulation – that inevitably presuppose linguistic formulation of thought. If translation as an activity confronts the person performing it with some difficulties, it does so because conceptualization is achieved by means of verbal articulation in the inner manner of shaping and formulation, but in the source language. If, on the other hand, the person translating has a good command of this type of activity (knowledge of the two languages is naturally taken for granted) conceptualization is achieved by means of the target language. That kind of conceptualization will be characterized by a high professional quality and it will be achieved through the inner, individual, object–scheme sense code.

In this way the first stage in the translation process is achieved by means of inner speech, but the ways in which it is achieved may differ, as may the degree to which it is achieved. That degree may be located anywhere between successive articulation, outwardly expressed, and simultaneous brain activity.

The second stage in the translation process is the stage in which the sense of the received utterance is established and its communicative content shaped. This stage can also be achieved under similar conditions, by means of the system of the source language, the system of the target language, or the object–scheme code. When conceptualization is achieved by means of the source language, however, a hiatus will develop between the sense of the message that has been received and the content of the message that has been reproduced, since reproduction must necessarily presuppose the system of the target language. It becomes necessary, therefore, to understand the relationship between sense and content. If they are to be adequately shaped it becomes necessary to "bring them together" and to reformulate them. The moment in which the switch from one language to another takes place will therefore occur in the second stage of the translation process.

If conceptualization is achieved in the target language, the shaping of the sense of the perceived utterance will also be the shaping of its communicative content. In that case, the very process of conceptualization already includes the reformulation of the means by which the perceived thought has been expressed. This process of reformulation is not a conscious one; rather it takes place as a highly automatized operation. Whenever conceptualization is a compressed, simultaneous process, automatic reformulation of the means by which the perceived thought is expressed is carried to the limit. As a result, the second stage, that of the content proper, presupposes a broad shaping of thought by means of the target language, free from interfering influences.

The third stage of the translation process is achieved in the outer manner of the shaping and formulation of thought by means of the target language. This third stage is the stage of the formulation of the utterance itself. If conceptualization is achieved by means of the inner manner of shaping and formulation of the source language, and if the sense of the perceived message is established and formulated in the source language as well, reformulation and the moment in which the switch occurs from one language to the other happen in the third stage, when thought is formulated.

These stages always follow each other in time in the case of any given portion of the message, or sense unit, but they can also co-exist in time and overlap during the processing of different portions of the message: while they conceptualize a given syntagma simultaneous translators are shaping and pronouncing the previous one. This fact seems to confirm that the two types of shaping and formulating thought (inner and outer speech) do indeed overlap. They overlap on different levels in different types of translation. Simultaneous interpretation, for instance, presupposes a simultaneous switching on of the two manners of shaping and formulating thought in the target language. Translation, on the other hand, is based on successive switching on of the inner manner of shaping and formulating thought in the source language during the process of conceptualization, followed by the shaping of the sense by means of the inner, individual, object–scheme code and the establishment of the correspondence between sense and content – in other words the shaping of the content of the utterance and the formulation of thought in the outer manner, by means of outer speech, in the target language.

It is only natural that each stage witnesses a much higher degree of perfection in the second case. Judged on the basis of the overlapping and intertwining of the manners of shaping and formulation of thought in the translation process simultaneous interpretation comes first, followed by consecutive interpretation and written translation.

The complex nature of translation as a type of speech activity is also highlighted by the fact that the deduction of the perceptive part of this activity, the product, becomes an object for its productive part. The deduction that is the result of conceptualization can achieve different levels depending on the conditions under which translation takes place. In the same way the object, or content, can be realized on different levels. Different types of translation differ in fullness and depth. Simultaneous interpretation is likely to achieve a minimum degree of fullness on the level of communicative content and this often results in a "breakdown of the program" (Leont'iev 1974b: 169). In written translation, on the other hand, both the content and the program of the utterance are pitched on the highest level.

I hope to have shown that translation represents a complex speech activity. Like other types of speech activity it is based on the manner in which thought is shaped and formulated by means of language, or speech. I consider translation an activity of speech, rather than thought, since it fulfills communicative, not cognitive, functions. Translation is an activity that helps achieve acts of communication. It is characterized by the same psychological content as other types of speech activity – all the more proof that it belongs among them.

If and when we consider translation as a specific type of speech activity, we may say that its specificity lies in its motivation. As is well known, all types of translation invariably meet truly personal needs of individuals, be they cognitive or communicative. This individual need has to "find itself" in the object of the speech activity, which is thought, and the need that has been objectivized in this way becomes the motive for the activity. In the process of translation man can fulfill his need to communicate with others. This primary social need in turn calls forth the cognitive–communicative need that seems to derive from the social need to receive information that has been adequately expressed in another language. It turns out that the object of the activity, namely thought received and reproduced, meets the social need by meeting the cognitive–communicative personal need called forth by that social need. Interestingly enough, the different types of translation can also be categorized according to this kind of motivation. Motivation tends to be most indirect in simultaneous interpretation, while the truly cognitive social motivation is least indirect in translation.

Still another specific feature of translation as a type of speech activity is the fact that this type of speech activity is initiated in its performative part by a different person. The performative part of an activity is the realization, the embodiment of the inner psychic image that is formed in the mind during the process of reflecting reality. In speech activity, particularly of the productive kind, such as speaking and writing, the image is presented in the form of its own content. In translation the content has been provided by another person. If image and action always find themselves in a relationship of inner correspondence in the speech activity known as speaking, for instance, the content provided by one person may fail to find in another person (the translator) an ability that is adequate to embody, shape, and formulate this initial content. It could be argued that both the motivation behind translation and the very activity of translating are indirect in nature. Moreover, the translator's activity succeeds in making the communicative act itself indirect in the act of translating. The elementary communicative act can be defined by the relationship between speaker and listener, reader and writer. The translator breaks up this direct relationship.

The specificity of translation as a type of speech activity is to be found first and foremost in its indirectness. On the level of the analysis of psychic processes such as memory, thought, perception, the specific nature of translation compared with other types of speech activity is revealed most obviously in the functioning of memory and in the reproductive character of thought. During the process of simultaneous interpretation operational memory carries the basic load: it preserves and stores not just what has been said, but also the decisions the translator has made, not to mention the translator's prognostication of what is about to be said. Reproductive thinking is basic to the two types of interpretation while translation is based on both productive and reproductive thinking. The translator's creative powers are therefore demonstrated most clearly in translation. These powers include not only "the constant search for linguistic tools to express the unity of form and content that makes up the original" (Fedorov 1968: 121) but also the establishing of "communicative equivalence between the texts of the original and the translation ... based on the functional equalization of those texts in both form and content" (Komissarov 1975: 46–7).

It is not enough to mention only the complexity of translation as a type of speech activity, or its specificity; one must also draw attention to its secondary nature.

The secondary nature of translation as a type of speech activity resides mainly in the fact that it is based on two other types of speech activity (listening and reading on the one hand, speaking and writing on the other). Moreover, translation's complex and specific nature represents a bringing together of the inner mechanisms of these types of speech activities, rather than their sum total. Translation therefore combines, to a different degree of amalgamation, the mechanisms of sense perception, sense expression, probability prognostication, and cataphoric synthesis. Moreover, any stage in one of these processes is likely to overlap with the subsequent stage:

understanding of sense is at the same time shaping of content. Experimental data taken from Benediktov's analysis have also revealed some structural characteristics of this activity, especially in the case of simultaneous interpretation. They serve to confirm his hypothesis that "since they happen simultaneously, listening and speaking exhibit the structure of a homogeneous activity. That activity can be defined as the simultaneous perception and reproduction of speech material" (1974b).

Proof that translation is not the sum of two types of speech activity but rather an autonomous, secondary type of this activity is provided by the fact that the subtypes operational in the process of translation have goals of their own. The goal of the receptive stage is understanding for the purpose of reproduction; the goal of the reproductive stage is the reproduction of what has already been understood.

The analysis of the psychological content of translation as a type of speech activity given here reveals the complexity and the specific nature of this speech activity. It also strengthens the conviction that a person who has mastered the basic types of speech activity will not necessarily turn out to be a good translator. Rather, translation needs to be taught by means of special methods that take the peculiar psychological characteristics of this complex, specific, secondary type of human speech activity into account.

WORKS CITED

Anokhin, P. (1969) *Biologiya i neirofiziologiya uslovnogo refleksa* [*The Biology and Neurophysiology of the Conditional Reflex*], Moscow: Medicina.

Belyaev, B. (1963) "Psihologicheskij analiz processa yazykovogovo perevoda" [A psychological analysis of the process of translation], *Inostrannye yazyki v vysshej shkole* [*Foreign Languages in High Schools*], vol. 2, Moscow: Rosvuzizdat, 150–70.

Benediktov, B. (1974a) *Psihologicheskij analiz odnovremennogo vospriyatiya i vosproiizvedeniya svyaznoi rechi* [*A Psychological Analysis of the Simultaneous Perception and Generation of Connected Speech*], Vil'njus: Vyshejshaya shkola.

——(1974b) *Psihologiya ovladeniya inostrannym yazy'kom* [*The Psychology of Learning a Foreign Language*], Minsk: Vyshejshaya shkola.

Fedorov, A. (1968) *Osnovy obshtej teorii perevoda* [*A Foundation for a General Theory of Translation*], Moscow: Vysshaya shkola.

Komissarov, V. (1975) "O dvoyakom podhode k izucheniyu perevodcheskoj deyatel'nosti" [On the binary approach to the study of translational activity], *Materialy vsesoyuznoi nauchnoi konferencii "Teoriya perevoda i nauchnye osnovy podgotovki perevodchikov"* [*Proceedings of the National Scientific Conference on Translation Theory and the Scientific Basis for Teaching Translation*], Moscow.

Leont'iev, A. N. (1959) *Problemy razvitiya psihiki* [*Problems of Psychic Development*], Moscow: Agenciya po pechate "Novosti" Rossijskoj Sovetskoj Federacii Socialisticheskih Republik.

——(1969) *Psihologicheskie edinicy i porozhdenie rechevogo vyskazivaniya* [*Psychological Units and the Generation of Utterances*], Moscow: Nauka.

Pegacheva, Z. (1959) "Nekotorye psihologicheskye voprosy obucheniya ustnomu perevodu" [Some psychological problems of teaching interpretation], *Byulletin' kolokviuma po eksperimental'noj fonetike i psihologii rechi* [*Bulletin of the Colloquium in Experimental Phonetics and Speech Psychology*], vol. 2, Moscow: Izdatel'stvo Moskovskogo Gosudarstvennogo Pedagogicheskogo Instituta Inostrannyh Yazykov (MGPIIJ), 130–48.

Revzin, I. and Rozentsveig, V. (1962) "K obosnovaniju lingvisticheskoi teorii perevoda" [On the need for a linguistic theory of translation], *Voprosy yazykoznaniya* [*Problems of Linguistics*] 1.

Rubinstein, S. (1940) *Osnovy obshtej psihologii* [*The Foundations of General Psychology*], Moscow.

Vygotskij, L. (1934) *Myshlenie i rech* [*Thinking and Speech*], Moscow and Leningrad: Socegiz.

Zimnyaya, I. and Chernov, G. (1970) "K voprosu o roli veroyatnostogo prognozirovaniya v processe sinhronnogo perevoda" [On the problem of the role of probability prognostication in the process of simultaneous interpretation], *Voprosy teorii i metodiki prepodavaniya perevoda* [*Problems in the Theory and Methodology of Teaching Translation*], Moscow: Izdatel'stvo MGPIIJa.

——"Veroyatnostnoe prognozirovanie v processe sinhronnogo perevoda" [Probability prognostication in the process of simultaneous interpretation], *Predvaritel'nye materialy eksperimental'nyh issledovanij po psiholingvistike* [*Preliminary Materials from Experimental Studies in Psycholinguistics*], Moscow: Izdatel'stvo Institut a Yazykoznaniya Akademii Nauk SSSR [Publishing House of the Institute of Linguistics of the Academy of Sciences of the USSR].

Chapter 11

A cognitive approach to translation equivalence

Bistra Alexieva

Conceptualization is likely to become one of the key concepts in future thinking about translation, so much so, in fact, that it may even succeed in giving "equivalence" a new lease of life, albeit in a negative sense: namely that it is impossible for the author and the translator to conceptualize a situation in equivalent terms, especially in the case of situations remote in time (the dubbing of knights in the Middle Ages, for instance) or space (present-day wedding ceremonies in Polynesia). Not only do individuals (authors and translators) not conceptualize the same situation in the same way, languages tend not to do so either. Or rather, languages tend to select different features of a situation for "overt" expression. No author, no language, ever describes a situation in all its details. Rather, some kind of outline is sketched which is then left to evoke the full situation in the reader's mind, though not necessarily in precisely the way the author held it in his or her individual mind, or the language in its collective mind. The different features of a situation selected for overt expression usually do not correspond on the semantic level, to name but one of the levels of "old style" equivalence. Birds, for instance, "sit" in Bulgarian, whereas they "perch" in English. Indeed, literal translation of the overt features of a situation that have been selected may lead to confusion, rather than communication. In this case the translator (and his or her teacher) must be aware of a kind of "equivalence" that is operative on the level of language itself and cannot be segmented into any kind of constitutive elements whatsoever without both losing its own meaning and impeding communication whenever the segmented elements are likely to be reconstituted in another language. It is at this level that cognitive and contrastive linguistics intersect. Their yoking together may prove to be of great importance for the translation pedagogy of the future.

A. L.

THE TERM "TRANSLATION EQUIVALENCE"

The use of the term "translation equivalence" is one of the controversial issues in translation studies today. The term has been frowned upon by many eminent translation scholars. It has been described as "perverse" (Holmes, quoted in Bassnett 1980: 28) or as an "obstacle" because of its precise definition in mathematics (Van den Broeck, quoted in Bassnett 1980: 26). This type of objection is certainly legitimate if equivalence is taken to mean "complete identity," and if it is not further specified in terms of equivalence of *what* (*x*).

The meaning of the word equivalence can be described as "equal in value, measure, force, effect, significance." Based on the word's etymology, however, its first half can also be taken to mean "like." The *Random House Dictionary* gives "equal" as being derived, via Middle English, from the Latin "aequalis," meaning "equal, like." Likeness does not imply complete identity and therefore allows for degrees of approximation. Moreover, it not infrequently happens that one and the same term is used in two or more different branches of science with certain modifications of meaning so that it can stand for different, or slightly different, concepts. According to the same *Random House Dictionary* "impulse," for instance, is used in mechanics to denote something like *"the product of the average force acting on a body and the time* during which that action takes place, equivalent to the change in the momentum of the body produced by such a force." In electricity, on the other hand, it refers to *"a single, usually sudden flow* of current in one direction." Yet the use of the same string of letters and sounds in these two different branches of physics to denote two different concepts is not an obstacle to a felicitous realization of the communicative act, since each of these terminological uses is well defined. We therefore need to have equivalence more rigorously defined in translation theory; we do not need to invent another term.

The first step toward such a definition is taken as soon as we place "translation" in front of "equivalence," thereby signaling the specific nature of the phenomenon. The second, more important step consists of the efforts made by translation scholars to achieve a higher degree of precision in determining the "slot" filled by the *x* after equivalence – equivalence of what? Translation scholars more or less unanimously accept that a relationship of equivalence on the level of the *words* of source and target language is impossible, since "the semantic map of each language is different" (Weinreich 1963: 142). Approaches and opinions vary with regard to the other levels of the text, and the issue is still open. I would therefore suggest that the term "equivalence" be retained, that it should be taken to mean something like "optimum degree of approximation," and that our efforts should be directed toward a more rigorous definition of the term itself. This should allow us to determine what elements of the source language text and its reception may, and do, remain equivalent in the target language text and its reception, and under what circumstances.

PREVIOUS APPROACHES

The development of linguistics in general, and of macrolinguistics and text linguistics in particular, has helped translation scholars to better understand the issue of translation equivalence. That understanding has also been fostered by the development of the theory of interlingual communication. It can be said to have evolved along two different lines.

First, a distinction has been made between (i) different hierarchically related levels of form and content, (ii) sets of levels, particularly in the cognitive analysis of literary texts, and (iii) different layers and types of meaning (referential, pragmatic, and intralinguistic) according to the function(s) of a sign or combination of signs.

Second, a more dynamic approach has been elaborated. This approach takes the receiver into consideration and investigates the equivalence of the effect that source and target texts have on source and target receivers.

Progress has been made along the first line of investigation, not least because more rigorous procedures of analysis have been elaborated in pursuing it. Progress along the second line of investigation remains relatively insignificant, not only because no use has been made of form/content level analysis, but also because the study of the responses of source and target language receivers has not progressed beyond the intuitive level.

Attempts to study these responses have included the introduction of various concepts. The concepts of "background knowledge" and "experience" of the receivers of source and target texts were introduced to account for the difference between receptors caused by their belonging to two different linguistic and cultural communities. They have not so far, however, been incorporated into any more rigorous system of analysis, nor has any metalanguage for their description been elaborated.

Another concept, introduced mainly by E. A. Nida, is that of "channel capacity" (Nida and Taber 1969: 163). Channel capacity is discussed in terms of two dimensions: the difficulty of the message and its length. The core of the concept is constituted by the attempt to reduce difficulty by making explicit in the target text what was implicit in the source text. If and when that is achieved, the target text will fit the channel capacity of target language receivers more or less to the same extent that the source text fitted the capacity of source text receivers.

The very notion of "difficulty," however, is difficult to handle in any more rigorous manner, since difficulty may be caused by many factors. Difficulty may be related not only to specific differences in language and culture, but also to the complexity of the topic, the genre, and other elements. A more promising strategy would therefore be to tackle different types of "difficulty" separately.

In this paper I shall try to tackle one of the most important language-specific aspects of the "difficulty" of a text, namely its "explicitness : implicitness" features. These are discussed by Nida only as constituting a movement from implicitness to explicitness, as "filling out ellipsis" (Nida and Taber 1969: 167). Yet there are many instances in translation in which the opposite movement takes place, namely from explicitness to implicitness. Data collected so far suggest that a description of a scene or situation does not include all its features; nor does it include the relationships between those features. Rather, the selection of features for overt expression tends to vary across languages. Some of these features and relationships seem to be, or to once have been, more salient than others. This prominence is fixed in the ways in which different languages are used. In Russian the presence of a fly on the ceiling would normally be described by means of "Na potolke sidit muha" [A fly sits on the ceiling]. Bulgarian, on the other hand, would use "Na tavana e kaznala muha" [On the ceiling a fly has perched]. The normal way of describing a situation would obviously evoke a normal response to the text on the receiver's part. Any deviation from what is considered the normal description would imply additional meanings – mostly of a pragmatic nature – that the native speaker will recognize and interpret adequately. Obviously the preservation of the source text "naturalness" of description, or of any deviation from that naturalness, in the target text will be one of the conditions for ensuring the highest possible similarity of response to the two texts.

Equally obviously, we should not be satisfied with merely stating these cross-language differences in the selection of features for implicit/explicit expression and pointing out their relevance to the discussion of translation equivalence. Any attempt to account for the phenomenon will confront us with a number of questions. We shall have to ask ourselves what the reasons are for the differences in the selection of situational features and the relationships between them for overt expression. We shall also have to ask ourselves what kind of relationship exists between these differences, viewed as one aspect of the "difficulty" of a text, and the receiver's "channel capacity."

A SUGGESTION

A text may have the same, or approximately the same, effect on two receivers if they have the same, or approximately the same, channel capacity basically determined by their knowledge and experience of the world. In linguistic terms we would say that the functional content of the text as a hierarchically layered structure of different types of meaning, in which one type plays the dominant part, is verbalized by means of linguistic signs on different levels in such a way as to be interpretable and receivable by both receivers with the same degree of approximation. Such a high similarity in interpretation and retrieval is possible if the two receivers have the same or approximately the same knowledge and experience of the world *mapped in similar ways in terms of language*, if they belong to one and the same linguistic and cultural community. Language is not just a means of communication but also a reflection of the way we experience and know the world in terms of universal experiential and cognitive models, as members of the human species, and in terms of a specific application of those models, as members of a linguistic and cultural community.

If the two receivers belong to different linguistic and cultural communities we may expect that their mental pictures of a situation will be different because different salient features and relationships between them will have been selected for overt expression. A literal copy of the mapping of the situation in the source text and its transfer to the target text may often impede the latter's reception. The study of the specific ways in which universal cognitive and experiential models are employed in a particular language is highly relevant to translation theory and practice.

As a first step I shall try to define the major types of cognitive and experiential models discernible in the way we use language. The first major distinction needs to be made between cases when (i) the selectional description of a situation is executed within one domain (one-domain mapping) and when (ii) the situational elements and the relationships between them are compared with those of a situation in another domain (two-domain mapping).

In the case of one-domain mapping a further distinction should be made along the "iconicity" parameter. "Iconic mapping" occurs when the predication selected for the matrix comes intact to the intralinguistic level, and therefore to the surface structure, and only downgraded predications (mostly of the existential and property-assigning type) remain explicit, as in "John saw the ham sandwich on the table." "Non-iconic mapping" occurs when a further distinction can be drawn. On one side of the dividing line we find metonymy proper, when part of a predication is selected for explicit expression to represent the whole, as in "One waitress says to the other: 'The ham sandwich has spilled beer all over himself,' " in which only the second argument in the predication "The man who is eating a ham sandwich" has come to the surface. On the other side of the dividing line we find predicate-splitting mapping, when space/time/cause coordinates are taken out of the predicate and mapped separately to fill the gap that results from the implication of the first argument of the predication, mostly in the semantic roles of writer (speaker)/ perceiver (viewer) as in "Tonight sees the last episode of *Poldark.*"

In the case of two-domain mapping a further distinction should be made between "metaphorical mapping" and "image-schematic mapping." "Metaphorical mapping" is based on the similarity between an argument, predicate, or single feature from a predication referring to the first domain, and its counterpart in the second domain. The English expression "She cut his argument to ribbons," for instance, is obviously based on the metaphor "arguments are like constructs" (Lakoff and Johnson 1980: 99).

"Image-schematic mapping" is based on a more complicated type of relationship. The similarity obtains between a feature, a property of an object, its shape, for instance, and the path, the trajectory formed by it, in other words between something static and something dynamic, as in "The road ran down the hill" and "The boy ran down the hill."

The reason why translators find it difficult to achieve greater similarity in the effect that source and target texts have on source and target receivers respectively is that experiential and cognitive models are often used differently in the different linguistic and cultural communities with respect to area, scope, and time of operation and, most importantly, choice of the domain for comparison. There are differences, for instance, between English and Bulgarian in the metaphorical mapping based on the comparison between the world of men and the world of birds or other natural objects and phenomena in terms of their position in space. In English the position of the human body referred to as "sitting" can be used with reference to birds as well. Yet to English "There sits a bird in every tree" corresponds Bulgarian "Na vsyako durvo e katznala ptichka" [A bird is perched on every tree]. The same applies to the position of celestial bodies. The English "A silver of moon rose over the horizon, hardly large enough to make a path of light even when it sat right down on the water" corresponds to Bulgarian "Nad horizonta se izdigna tunuk lounen surp, bezsilen da propravi puteka ot svetlina dori kogato polegna na vodata" [when it lay down on the water]. The Bulgarian translation of the bird in the tree has been achieved by means of one-domain iconic mapping. The translation of the moon has been achieved by means of two-domain metaphorical mapping, with the comparison made to another position of the human body: "lying down" instead of "sitting."

In the case of the "arguments are like constructs" metaphor the mapping is similar but the specific constructs themselves are not the same, and this causes differences in the remaining part as well, since in Bulgarian the construct is reduced to dust, or ashes, as in "Tya napravi dovodite mou na puh i prah" [She reduced his arguments to fluff and dust].

In the case of one-domain mapping differences appear in the non-iconic types mainly along the following parameters. Sometimes a part is chosen to represent the whole. Compare English "There was music from my neighbor's house through the summer nights" with Bulgarian "Prez letnite noshti ot kushtata na suseda mi se chouvashe muzika/dolitashe muzika" [Through the summer nights music flew/was heard from my neighbor's house]. English explicitly renders the existential predication to signal the whole scene, including its perceptual and sound-propagating predications; in Bulgarian the whole is indicated by the explicit rendering of one of the latter.

Sometimes a certain part of the predicate can be taken out of the predicate splitting mapping and turned into an argument that surfaces as a subject. In Bulgarian, for instance, this kind of mapping works with the "place" coordinate. That coordinate can surface as a subject under certain conditions. Restrictions tend to be more severe in the case of the "time" coordinate: it cannot surface as a subject in "Tazi vecher shte vidim poslednata seria na Poldark" [Tonight we shall see the last episode of *Poldark*], which is nevertheless equivalent to the English "Tonight sees the last episode of *Poldark*." This type of mapping does not occur at all with the cause coordinate.

The use of cognitive and experiential modes can help us establish the relationship between the "real" scene (situation) in its entirety (with or without a comparison domain) and its "language- and culture-specific mental picture" that determines the intralinguistic level and therefore the surface structure which the addressee can interpret as signaling the whole. The idea that an extralinguistic situation is hardly ever described by explicitly expressing all its features and the relationships between them can now be defined more rigorously by means of the cognitive and experiential models that capture the universal and language-specific mechanisms governing the selection of the "implicit : explicit" configuration. In other words the selection of what is to be made explicit and what not depends not just on the speaker's communicative intentions but also on the way(s) in which cognitive and experiential models operate and are fixed in a specific language.

It is therefore possible to distinguish between "explicit : implicit" configurations caused by the speaker's intentions, which can be assigned to the sub-level of pragmatic meaning, and the "explicit : implicit" configuration caused by language-specific ways of employing the universal cognitive and experiential models, a configuration that is valid for all native speakers of the language and can therefore be assigned to the sub-level of intralinguistic meaning.

The most important consequence of such an approach is that it becomes possible to capture at least *part* of the source and target text receivers' knowledge and experience that determines their response to the source and target texts and to introduce it – albeit indirectly – into the semantic structure via the appropriateness/inappropriateness of the "implicit : explicit" configuration on the sub-level of intralinguistic meaning. In other words, the "explicit : implicit" configuration on the intralinguistic level in source and target texts that is the result of a given type of language- and culture-specific mapping can help us predict the degree of similarity in the effect that source and target texts can have on their receivers. This is particularly valid in the case of artistic writing since the creation of new images is usually intimately related to, and based on, language- and culture-specific mappings.

CONCLUSIONS

These first steps toward using a cognitive approach to translation equivalence suggest that the strategy of tackling the issue in terms of "equivalence of source and target language receivers' responses" is a promising one indeed, and that this response can be more rigorously defined by resorting to content level analysis based on the distinction between "explicit : implicit" configurations on the pragmatic and intralinguistic sub-levels of the deep semantic structure determined by the language- and culture-specific ways in which universal cognitive and experiential models are applied.

I shall also venture to suggest that two texts can be defined as translationally equivalent if the functional content of the source text as a hierarchically layered structure of different types of meaning, in which one type plays the dominant part, is rendered in the target text in such a way as to fit the cognitive and experiential models (types of mapping) typical of target language usage in the production of a text, and therefore ensures a reception by the target language receiver of the functional content of the source text that is the same, or approximately the same, as the source text receiver's reception of that functional content.

WORKS CITED

Bassnett, Susan (1980) *Translation Studies*, London and New York: Methuen (revised edn, 1991).
Lakoff, G. and Johnson, M. (1980) *Metaphors We Live By*, Chicago, IL: University of Chicago Press.
Nida, E. A. and Taber, C. (1969) *The Theory and Practice of Translation*, Leiden: Brill.
Weinreich, U. (1963) "On the semantic structure of language," in J. Greenberg (ed.) *Universals of Language*, Cambridge, MA: MIT Press.

Chapter 12

Sense and its expression through language

Leonora Chernyakhovskaya

Translators make sense of the texts they translate from language A and then re-express that sense in language B. But what is it that allows them to make sense? Does sense pre-exist language? Do human beings share in "sense" before that shared sense is taken away from them by different languages and obscured by words and phrases?

Again, these are questions that Western thinking about translation tends not to touch but leaves to philosophers, often with an almost audible sigh of relief. Russian scholars of translation, on the other hand, while not exactly rushing into this part of the field, do not totally neglect it either.

Because they are not as familiar with current Western philosophy of science, not to mention philosophy of philosophy, as their colleagues in the West, Russian translation scholars tend to be more unabashedly certain of the existence, or at least the putative existence, of "something" that, quite literally, "makes" sense. This position puts them at odds with most of current Western ironic relativism, which does not set great store by any attempt to actually come to know what sense "is," and simply assumes "sense" as the product of a given culture at a given time.

Almost paradoxically, given their ideological point of departure, their point of view is much closer to the kind of hermeneutics practiced by the later Heidegger and the later Wittgenstein. In these neo-hermeneutic terms the translators' "being in the world" as translators allows them to have their own say about sense, precisely from the vantage point of their particular "being in the world." There is no guarantee that what they say about sense will actually be seen to make sense, but there is also no reason why they should not be allowed to say it, to allow their own truth to become manifest in the words that are inspired by their practice.

A. L.

The word "sense" is applied widely in various fields of science. In logic it is mainly used to name the invariant in synonymic expressions, the "something" that remains unchanged in spite of various kinds of paraphrasing.

In psychology the word "sense" is used to name semantic fields connected with the personal interpretation of words, combinations of words, events, and human behavior in fields of association aroused by the same words in different people.

Linguistics is interested in sense as the object expressed by language and through language. Linguistics is interested in the correlation between the sense expressed through language and the meaning of the signs of language, the correlation between the system of concepts and the system of signs. It is also interested in the correlation between what is said in speech and the linguistic means that produce speech, the correlation between what is said and the way in which it is said, the way the signs of a language are arranged into speech structures both grammatical and semantic. In other words, linguistics is interested not only in the sense of words, combinations of words, and other linguistic units, but also in the sense of concrete texts. I shall be referring to the latter sense in this paper.

I contend that the sense of the text has a psychic origin, that it is the result of mental activity, that it represents an "ideational" product.

I consider the ideational to be the product of the interaction of two kinds of matter: organic, biologically alive matter, such as the socially developed brain, and the matter of the surrounding world that influences the brain.

The resulting phenomenon is neither the first nor the second kind of matter, but something else, the result of the interaction between the two. There is an analogy to this in mathematical logic where the correlation of two objects is taken to be an object as well, but an object of a higher logical rank than the two objects correlated.

The ideational is both the process and the product of the process. Both the product and the process present us with a model of the surrounding world – a specific model.

Traditionally a model has been defined as a system of interconnected elements that represents the most essential peculiarities of the object that is being modeled in other materials: the structure of the object is represented by means of some other material arranged to reproduce the essential features of the original.

The ideational product is not matter of any kind: it is just function. We therefore cannot refer to any material in which the model of the surrounding world is represented, but only to two kinds of matter: the matter of the brain and the matter of the surrounding world. These two produce the function when they enter into reciprocal action. They are both viewed not as materials for modeling but as types of conditions for it, as its substratum, its material bearer, the necessary condition of its existence.

Each of the components in the action may serve as the ideational's substratum. The ideational may therefore have either biologically alive matter as its substratum (the brain), or any kind of specifically organized matter around the brain. In the first case the ideational is based on the biological substratum; it therefore remains within the mind of the individual who has been producing it. In the second case it is separated from the individual.

It is possible to maintain that the ideational product has several forms of existence. One of them is the actually ideational, a psychical experience that occurs during the process of accepting information provided either by the outer world or by memory.

Another form is the *potentially ideational.* The potentially ideational can be said to exist either on the basis of a biological substratum (the brain), as the subconscious, in the memory, or on the basis of some other material substratum outside the brain. In that case it is separated from the individual and it exists as a specifically organized system: a picture, a sculpture, a drawing, a text.

One more form of the ideational is the *virtually ideational* processing of information in the sphere of the subconscious.

The content of the ideational product, the model of the world, can be said to be a transformed form of the world. The concept of the transformed form has been introduced into philosophy by Ludwig Feuerbach. It is now used to characterize a certain way in which complicated systems function. The concept of the transformed form mainly holds that the shape of some material content achieves independence under certain conditions, separates from that content and melts into the specific features of the new material that serves as a substratum for that shape – as in the case of symbolism, for instance.

If we decide to make use of the concept of the transformed form we can define information as an ideational product, the transformed form of the real world, the world of quasi-objects or, in other words, the world of knowledge. The social development of *homo sapiens*, which is the product of experience, is such a world, shaped as the result of the cognitive and creative activity of individuals united in a society. I shall proceed to call the content of this world, the world of social knowledge, "cognitive information," and I shall take it to mean the world of the ideational that has been coded by means of certain material systems. Social knowledge represents the potentially ideational on the basis of a material substratum outside the brain. Uniformity of physiological mechanisms of perception and the availability of a basic ideational product accumulated as the result of the mental activities and the social experience of many generations provide for the unity of the image of the world, the unity of social knowledge.

Social knowledge can be contrasted with individual knowledge. Individual knowledge is the result of the cognitive and creative processes of individuals, their own image of the world experienced as their own psychical experience, but nevertheless shaped under the influence of the real world and the world of social knowledge. Individual knowledge represents the potentially ideational on the basis of the biological substratum.

Individual knowledge as potentially ideational (the memory, the subconscious) may transfer into the virtually ideational when information is processed by the subconscious, or into the actually ideational when conscious thinking takes place.

If we accept the concepts of the potentially, the virtually, and the actually ideal, the concept that allows us to separate the ideational from a biological substratum and to move it to a non-biological material substratum also allows us to look on the ideational product not just as a form of human activity but also as its separated result, the potentially ideational on the basis of a material substratum, ready to turn into its actual, or at least virtual state when it comes into contact with the human brain.

The social experience that accumulates ideational products has been fixed in language. Language is not genetically inherited; it is acquired during a lifetime. Since language itself is both social and individual knowledge, it may be considered part of the social knowledge, the element that stores, develops, and exchanges social knowledge. A very special feature of language is its double existence. It exists on the basis of both biological and non-biological material (sound, letters) substrata. On the basis of its material substratum it exists, as social knowledge, in the shape of signs and the verbally formulated rules for their usage; on the basis of its ideological substratum it functions both consciously and subconsciously for its bearer, and there is no direct evidence of the exact form of its functioning. The only evidence we have up to now suggests that it functions via some bioelectric nervous codes, different at different stages of thinking, speaking, and apprehending other people's speech.

The fact that language has two forms of existence based on two kinds of substrata is of great importance. Language may be looked on as a "bridge," a spanning device that helps to separate the developing ideational product from the biological substratum into the outer world. Language provides the material in which the ideational product is modeled when it is separated from the interacting material systems, the brain and the outer world, that gave birth to it.

The ideational product developed on the basis of the biological substratum is the result of human beings' creative activity and it is made possible by their previous social experience. The product is formed, or modeled, in some kind of language-related shape on the basis of the biological stratum. These shapes are obviously not always necessarily verbal in the traditional meaning of that word; they may also include visual thinking, or thinking in images. They are then transferred into linguistic signs, specifically organized on the basis of the sound or graphic substratum.

The transfer from one substratum to another entails a serious change in the material of the modeling. This change is further compounded by the existence of the specific features of any national language that may also influence the peculiar characteristics of the product that is modeled by this or that national language. It is common knowledge that certain peculiar features of the material in which the object is modeled cannot but influence the model.

Therefore, if individuals intend to produce a certain text, if they have a certain idea, a certain ideational product to be separated from their consciousness, the text that is the result of this activity will somehow be influenced by the particular language through which the ideational product is to be "materialized."

The ideational product produced by human beings and separated from them by means of a national language is precisely what

I would like to call "sense." This means that the sense of the text is always the same, no matter what national language is used to separate it from the individual. At the same time the sense would depend in some of its particular features on some specific features of the national language by means of which it has been separated from the individual.

Once the sense has been separated, and once it has been brought to life in the shape of a text, it is considered potentially ideational, and it will remain so until it comes into contact with another human, socially developed brain. That contact will turn it into the actually ideational, and the quality of the actually ideational product will depend on the degree of individual knowledge present in the potential receiver.

Our ideal should be to study the ideational product as it completes its trajectory from the moment of its birth to the moment of its separation and constitution as a text, but that seems hardly possible at present. The only alternative, therefore, is to follow the trajectory along which sense, the actually ideational, is produced by a text that comes into contact with a receiver. I have elaborated a special method for doing so and I shall now proceed to list its major elements.

Assuming the receiver has sufficient background knowledge, any text that is brought into contact with a receiver produces a certain psychical reflection of extralinguistic reality as planned by the author of the text. The degree of exactness of the reflection depends on the extent of the receiver's background knowledge.

The smallest unit of the text that produces a segment of that psychical reflection, irrespective of the rest of the text, is considered the "predicative unit," or PU. The PU is a combination of two signs that belong to language. It is the function of one sign to identify, to name single objects; it is the function of the other to classify the objects by assigning some attribute or property to them.

The PU must contain information not just about the name of an object and its properties, but also about the necessary parameters of its correlation with extralinguistic reality: information about the fact of its existence (the seme of being), its temporal and spatial location, the degree of reality of its existence in the world.

The PU represents a linguistic projection of a segment of extralinguistic reality into the knowledge of a potential receptor. Its obligatory components therefore include the name of the object, the names of its attribute or attributes, the presence of the seme of "being," and the modal, spatial, and temporal evaluation of the object.

Some of these components may not be formally present within the PU but they may be implied by the previous context or they may be known to receivers because of their background knowledge. But if at least one of the components within a word combination is neither formally expressed nor present in the receiver's background knowledge, that word combination is not considered a PU, but rather a pseudo-predicative unit, or PPU. A PPU does not produce any segment of the reflection of extralinguistic reality. The word combination "a red flower," without any further context, would be considered a PPU. Within a context it may become a PU, as when there would be a vase full of red and yellow flowers and one of the people looking at the vase would say: "Will you give me a red flower?" In this case "a red flower" implies something like "one of the red flowers from the vase you have in front of you right now."

Some of the obligatory components of the PU may therefore not be formally expressed within the PU itself, but they may be implied by a narrow context (of which the PU is itself a component) or a wide context (the receptor's background knowledge, the actual situation).

If all the necessary components of a PU are formally present within the PU that PU represents an extensive predication.

Consider the sentence: "*A conference on humanitarian aid to Kampuchea* was held at UN headquarters in New York on November 5, 1980." In this sentence the naming of an object (in italics) is correlated with extralinguistic reality by means of all the obligatory parameters expressed in the same sentence.

If some of the necessary components are not formally present in the PU but are implied by the context, that PU is called a "curtailed predication."

In the sentence "*The South African Government* is set to implement the policy of 'liberalizing' the racist regime," the combination of words in italics is a curtailed PU. Without the context it would not possess the necessary parameters for existence as a PU, such as the temporal and modal parameters that are supplied within the context of the whole sentence.

If a PU is represented only by a name that serves to identify and if the obligatory components of the PU are implied by the context or by the potential receiver's background knowledge, we are faced with a "zero predication." Zero predication may be contextual when the obligatory parameters are supplied by the context, or noncontextual if they are supposed to be supplied by the potential receiver's background knowledge. Geographical names, for instance, dates, the names of famous people may be introduced into the text as pure namings without further information concerning their spatial and temporal relationship.

If the identifier has been supplied within the text with all the necessary parameters for correlating the name of an object with the object in extralinguistic reality, the identifier is considered a "domineering name" that correlates with a definite object in extralinguistic reality in all other cases when it, or its substitute, is used, even if no obligatory components for such a correlation are present. In the segment "A little boy entered the room where his parents were watching TV. The boy said ..." "the boy" is considered a curtailed PU, whereas "a little boy" is merely a name within an extensive PU.

A text may be divided into units larger than the PU. The appearance of a new domineering name generally serves as a sign of a borderline within a text. In the example just given the borderline divides two sentences. It can also run through a single sentence like "In front of the picture stood a little man who suddenly started talking rather loudly." The borderline here runs between "a little man" and "who." It separates the first portion of the text, an extensive PU, from the next one that begins with the substitute for "a little man." In this case the substitute "who" is a domineering name and its appearance indicates the beginning of a new segment of text.

Other criteria for distinguishing segments of a text are temporal and spatial parameters. A change of at least one of them signals the beginning of a new segment of the text, as in "Once upon a time there lived a king. He was young and strong. One day he decided ... ."

A segment of the text that produces a segment of the reflection of an extralinguistic reality that has permanent spatial and temporal parameters and does not contain a new domineering name will be called an utterance. Utterances are text units that are linguistic projections of extralinguistic reality into the mind of the receptor. If PUs are a text's atoms, utterances are its molecules. They produce rather independent segments of a reflection of extralinguistic reality produced by the whole text.

The following procedure is followed in the analysis of a text for the purpose of establishing its sense. The analyzed text is divided into utterances. Within the utterances all nouns are singled out and numbered. If a noun has an attribute, the whole word combination is treated as a complex name. The nouns are then grouped into the minimum word combinations they form in the utterances within the text. These word combinations are treated as complex names and grouped into more complex word combinations with other nouns isolated in the utterances, and this process is repeated until exhausted.

Within the utterance "Five mark commemorative coins with the portrait of Otto Hahn, a famous German physicist, were minted in West Germany for the hundredth anniversary of his birth," the minimum word combinations are "five mark commemorative coins," "Otto Hahn, a famous German physicist," "his birth" (because "his" is a substitute for Otto Hahn). These word combinations, classified as complex names, are grouped into combinations with other names. The principle of word grouping remains constant: a name in the identifying function is always classified together with a name in the classifying function. In the combination "five mark commemorative coins" the complex name "commemorative coins" is used as an identifier, while the complex name "five marks" classifies the identifier. The next level of word combinations includes "the portrait of Otto Hahn, a famous German physicist." The word "portrait" is the identifier of the group; "five mark commemorative coins with the portrait" is the complex name, and "five mark commemorative coins" is the identifier within the group.

The identifier–classifier groups are subjected to componential analysis. This enables us to establish which of the word combinations include all the necessary components of a PU and which word combinations are to be treated as PPUs only.

The word combination that includes all the obligatory components of a PU (irrespective of its syntactic shape: a sentence, an attributive complex, or just a name) is considered a segment of the psychical reflection of the extralinguistic reality produced by the text under analysis.

This method makes it possible to follow the trajectory taken by the generalized meaning of separate words as they are transformed into the concrete function of naming an extralinguistic object or, in other words, the transformation of generalized meaning into concrete sense produced by the text.

The structure of the PUs is strictly limited to each individual text and never repeated in another text. Yet if we compare the analysis of the original text and of its translation we see that the two texts exhibit approximately the same hierarchical structure, with the degree of exactness of their correspondence depending on the degree of exactness of the translation. The correspondence between the structures of the two texts is due to the fact that the texts have the same content, the same sense, even though they have been produced by means of different languages.

The method described here enables us to evaluate the level of translation, and its closeness to the original, at least in preserving the structure and the sense of the text. Beyond that it also allows us to single out the sense structure and to study its peculiarities irrespective of the particular linguistic means used to produce it.

A comparative analysis of the same text in two languages, the original and its translation, makes it possible to single out two types of segments of the psychical reflection of extralinguistic reality. These types differ in the quality of information they contain. The first type, called "monorheme," contains information both about the object named as a segment of a reflection of extralinguistic reality, and about the obligatory parameters for correlating the object named with extralinguistic reality. Information about these parameters is usually introduced in a non-contextual way and it is oriented toward the average level of the potential receiver. It is usually presented in the form of names (mostly geographical names and data). This kind of information is called a non-contextual theme (NCT). Naming the reflected segment of reality in combination with the seme of "being" is a "rheme" (R). NCT and R are the two components of the monorheme.

The second type of text segment that reflects extralinguistic reality is called a "derheme." In the derheme the segment usually introduced by the monorheme is defined according to its attributes. This information on the attributes represents the segment's rheme. Its theme is a semantic repetition of a previously introduced reflection segment, and it is called a "contextual theme" (CT).

These two types of reflection segments are produced by different means in Russian and in English. Text analysis along the lines suggested here allows us to investigate the different ways in which monorhemes and derhemes are produced in both English and Russian.

The sense structure of the text established as a result of this analysis reveals that sense structure is non-linear, non-discrete in nature, although this does not hold true for text segments that reflect extralinguistic reality since these segments are tightly interconnected within the hierarchy they constitute.

This non-linear sense structure is the structure of the actually ideational product produced in the mind of any receiver of the text who possesses adequate knowledge.

When the actually ideational has to be transferred back into a potentially ideational state it has to be turned back into a chain of discrete language signs. Where translation of the text into another language is concerned, that text will have to be turned into another chain of other signs. What exactly is the difference if we transfer from Russian into English, for instance?

If the psychic reflection of reality produced by specifically organized language signs is a non-linear, non-discrete ideational product, its change into a specially organized system of the signs of another language must contain elements capable of dissecting it into discrete units and placing those units in a linear chain.

Functional sentence perspective (FSP) appears to be a good way to achieve such a transformation. The division of texts into utterances tends to reflect the division of the psychic reflection into segments produced by certain sets of linguistic means at the moment when the text is perceived. The division of utterances into theme and rheme may reflect the division of a segment into "pieces" of sense necessary for their linear representation. The presence of a certain semantic word order, equal or different in different languages, may reflect the actual moment of their linear representation. In Russian and English derhemes, for instance, the theme always opens the utterance and the rheme always closes it. In monorhemes, on the other hand, the semantic word order is strictly opposite in Russian and English. The presence of NCTs allows the necessary evaluation of the rheme with regard to extralinguistic reality to take place. The presence of CTs provides for semantic ties between the semantic groups that follow each other in a line: it provides for the semantic coherence of the text. The syntactic shape of these semantic groups is determined by the peculiarities of a national language.

As a transitional moment FSP contains some logical elements because it reflects the structure of the ideational product of thinking irrespective of the concrete linguistic means of its expression. At the same time it is impossible to analyze FSP outside of linguistics since it is obviously FSP itself that provides for the transfer of the ideational product from the biological substratum to the outer material substratum, and since it is only on the second substratum that both language and the separated ideational product become available for objective study.

There are various sets of grammatical means that make it relatively easy to establish the presence of FSP in various languages. But these sets transfer what is general for any language: the sense structure of the psychic reflection, individual for every particular case of reflection, but arranged according to some principles common for every reflection produced by linguistic means. The initial moment of transfer of psychic reflection into text is probably also common for different texts, irrespective of the language in which they are produced.

Chapter 13

Realia in translation

Sider Florin

Russian and Bulgarian thinking about translation has traditionally devoted more time and more words to the problem of what Russian and Bulgarian translation scholars usually refer to as "realia," those elements (things like "samovars," for instance, or concepts like "samizdat") in the original that are intimately bound up with the universe of reference of the original culture.

Realia are important for at least two reasons. They show quite unequivocally that translation, though based in language, is by no means limited to language. Translators have to transfer things and concepts from one universe of reference to another, not just words from one language to another. Realia also show that translations are, and will always remain, translations. No matter how elegant the different strategies proposed to "solve" the problem of realia, that problem remains without any definitive solution in the end: samovars will always remain samovars, and never really become transposed kinds of stoves. Realia constitute those points in the translated text at which "the translation is showing," simply because the universe of reference of culture A never totally overlaps with the universe of reference of culture B.

Realia show that translation as an attempt to bridge the gap between languages and cultures can always be only that: an attempt. As such, they affirm the "otherness" of the original in the midst of the most idiomatic use of the target language. This used to be a problem in the days when translations were supposed to be mere "windows" on the world of the other, transparent artifacts that would allow readers of the translation to enter the world of the original without even noticing that they had crossed a boundary somewhere.

An alternative view of realia is that they are not transparent glass, but that they reveal the way in which the glass that allows, or allowed, the author of the original and his or her first audience to look at their own world has been cut, polished, and crafted.

A. L.

If we strip a *cowboy* of his traditional garb and attire him in the *burnous* of a Sahara shepherd he will lose all his natural semblance and turn into an Arab. If we make a *geisha* change her loose and airy *kimono* for a Tyrolean *dirndl* with a close fitting bodice there will be nothing Japanese left in her. On the other hand, it is possible to take a bath in a *sauna* anywhere in Europe, but that bath will be called Finnish, not Turkish or Russian. There is a great difference between an ancient Roman *toga* and the *togas* judges wear in some countries. India has *jungles*, South Africa has a *veld*, and Siberia has its *taiga*.

All this and much more brings us to the subject of local and/or historical color, closely connected with the problem of background knowledge. I consider this the most important problem in literary translation in our day, when the barriers of distance and time have dwindled to insignificance in some cases, but become even more important in others. The bulk of that background knowledge we expect the general reader to possess or acquire consists of *realia*.

Realia (from the Latin *realis*) are words and combinations of words denoting objects and concepts characteristic of the way of life, the culture, the social and historical development of one nation and alien to another. Since they express local and/or historical color they have no exact equivalents in other languages. They cannot be translated in a conventional way and they require a special approach.

Realia may be classified thematically, according to the material or logical groups they belong to; temporally, according to the historical period they belong to; and geographically, according to the locations in which they are used.

The thematic category may be divided into more sub-categories. Ethnographical realia belong to everyday life, work, art, religion, mythology, and folklore. Examples would be *sarong, sombrero, moccasin,* and *fibula; bungalow, igloo,* and *wigwam; amphora* and *gyuvetch; rickshaw, fellah,* and *gaucho; kolkhoz* and *Senn; tarantella, reel, blues, canzonetta, commedia del arte* and *Kasperl, yule log, First of May,* and *Valentine*. Ethnographic realia also include purely ethnic realia like

Basque, Comanche, and Cossack; Schwabe, gringo, Boche, and cockney. We could also add measurements like *ell, verst, Morgan,* and *Pfund,* together with currency units like *dime, Groschen,* and *halfpence.*

Another thematic sub-category is that of social and territorial realia: *shire, state,* and *canton; corso* and *agora; Storting* and *Knesset; Kanzler, khan, sheriff,* and *alcalde; Ku Klux Klan, Roundheads, hayduts, prohibition,* and *NEP; fan* and *hippie.* There is a host of other categories, groups, and sub-groups that would go far beyond the confines of this contribution.

Geographical categories are obvious, at first: the Norwegian *fjord,* the Hungarian *puszta,* the Arabian *simoom,* the Dutch *polder,* and the Sherpa *yeti.* Beyond this, further classification of geographical realia is quite relative, depending on whether the criteria for their national characteristics belong to the source or target language. The most expedient classification appears to be not strictly territorial but language based, that is, based on whether or not the realia belong to only one or to both of the languages mentioned above.

Realia that belong to one language only may be divided into *national* realia, such as *borschcht* for the USSR and *goulash* for Hungary, *Punch and Judy* for England, and *Kasperl* for Germany; *local* realia, such as *Senner* for the Austrian and Bavarian Alps, and *artel* for the USSR; *microlocal* realia, such as *Heurige* for Vienna and *Lord Mayor's Show* for London; *international* realia that were national in origin but have been adopted by many languages, such as *sombrero, canoe, skyscraper,* and *regional realia* that do not necessarily occur in neighboring language zones, such as *pasha* for the countries of the Middle East, *haji* for the whole of the Muslim world, and *voivoda* for Bulgaria and Yugoslavia.

When translating within the scope of the source language and/or the target language, we can easily divide realia into the type that belongs to one language and is alien to the other, and the type that is alien to both languages. In a translation from Norwegian into any other language, or vice versa, *fjord* will belong to the former type; it will belong to the latter type in a translation from or into any language other than Norwegian.

From the point of view of time, realia may be most conveniently divided into the *modern* and the *historical* categories. This elementary classification is complicated, however, by the interdependence of object and time, as in the case of helmet in a medieval as opposed to a modern source text, and by the interdependence of place and time, as in the case of *toga* mentioned above, where a distinction has to be made between the ancient Roman garment and the modern judge's robe.

A final consideration should be that of the degree of acceptability of realia in the target language. Some realia are accepted in the target language and included in its vocabulary; others are felt as comparatively new in the target language and are rarely used; yet others are transitory and short lived, traversing the trajectory from modern to obsolete at great speed.

Realia do not always keep their historical status either: we may see historical realia turning into technical and other terms, while other terms may gradually turn into realia. It is enough to open any technical dictionary to find both examples on every page.

This minute and yet far from complete classification of realia brings us to another, more important point: their translation.

In its strict sense the term "translation" is inapplicable to realia since realia are untranslatable as a rule and are therefore introduced into a text by means other than translation proper. The main difficulties likely to beset any attempt at translating realia are the absence of equivalents or analogs in the target language and the need to communicate the objective meaning of realia to the target reader along with their local or historical color, or connotation.

This leaves really only two ways in which realia can be communicated to the target reader: transcription on the one hand, and substitution on the other. Transcription amounts to little more than a mechanical transfer of realia from source to target language by graphic means. In translations from languages using the Latin alphabet into languages using the Cyrillic alphabet, for instance, the transcription involves transliteration. In translations from languages using the Cyrillic alphabet into languages using the Latin alphabet, or from one language using the Cyrillic alphabet into another using that same alphabet, as in translations from Russian into Bulgarian, for instance, transcription is based on the phonetic principle. This is the easiest and therefore not always the most satisfactory method.

In all other cases, when transcription is considered unsuitable, undesirable, or even impossible, realia are introduced by means of several kinds of substitutions.

Translators may *introduce neologisms*, which may be calques, or translation loan words. In the case of composite words or idioms substitution takes place for each component: the Russian *udarnik* becomes *shock worker* and the Bulgarian *Narodno Sobranye* becomes *National Assembly*. Alternatively, calques may be combined with a target language element, as in *the Third Reich* for *das Dritte Reich*. In other cases the calque is assimilated into, or adapted to, the target language by means of flexion and/or affixation, as in English *stakhanovite* for Russian *stakhanovets*. Finally, nearly every translator has at least once introduced a semantic neologism or a newly minted compound word into his or her mother tongue. These neologisms or new compounds usually come into being on an etymological basis other than that of the source language word.

A more widely used method is probably that of *approximate translation*. In this case the general, rather than the exact, content of the realia is communicated, with the unavoidable result that local and/or historical color is always lost. General denotations may be substituted for specific denotations in this case: "a glass of *mineral water*," for instance, may be used to translate "a glass of *vichy*."

Alternatively, translators may rely on the use of functional equivalents, or analogues. They may try to achieve a reaction on the part of the reader of the translation that they consider similar to the reaction of the reader of the original. They may also substitute a convenient or familiar object or concept for an inconvenient or unknown one: one kind of flower, for instance, or game is easily substituted for another.

Descriptions or explanations are used only when it is impossible to render realia in any other way. They do not render the actual realia, but rather their meaning, or content, as dictionaries do.

Finally, translators also resort to *contextual translation*. This kind of translation is characterized by the absence of any correspondence with the translated word or words. Their content or meaning is communicated by means of a context suitably transformed as in the case of many new concepts current in the socialist countries that are totally unknown in other states. This method obviously only succeeds in communicating the general meaning: all local color is lost.

This long list of different methods would be without any practical value if it were left unsupplemented by further considerations governing the choice of the method most suited to each particular case. Translators are always confronted by the dilemma: transcribe or substitute? Which method is more likely to ensure minimum loss combined with maximum communication? The choice they make also depends on various premises.

It may be connected with *the character of the text*. In this case the choice depends on the generic features of texts. In scientific texts realia are terms, and translated as such. In literary works transcription is possible in works of a narrative nature, since transcription can be combined with the use of the footnote – a strategy manifestly impossible in drama. Solutions may be different in the translation of a short story and in the translation of a novel. In books for children it is advisable to eschew transcription and to explain the unfamiliar realia in the text itself. In adventure books transcription sometimes becomes a desirable exotic element. In books of popular science exhaustive commentaries and glossaries are most definitely admissible.

Choice may also be connected with the *importance of the realia in the context*. This may well be the main consideration for translators trying to decide between transcription and substitution. Translators have to evaluate whether in any given case realia are close to the source reader's center of attention or whether they count more as details. Realia that are alien to the source language tend to stand out and the author of the original has to explain them to the reader in some way. Realia that belong to the source language but are alien to the target language are much more difficult to discern and translators will find it hard to decide how they should be introduced into their translations.

Alternatively, choice may be connected with the *nature of the realia*. In this case translators will have to take the characteristics of the realia as lexical units in the systems of source and target languages into account. They will have to decide on the basis of the realia's relative familiarity, or lack of it, the literary tradition, the language register, the thematic, geographical, or temporal categories to which they belong.

Choice may further be connected with the *peculiar characteristics of source and target languages*, such as their grammar, the combinatorial possibilities governing word formation, the relative acceptability of calques or lack thereof.

Finally, choice may be connected with the *reader of the translation*. Which factors characterize the "average reader" of the target text and how do they compare with analogous factors characterizing the "average reader" of the source text? Translators translate for their readers and no communication has been established if readers fail to understand the realia that have been transcribed. If translators introduce realia by other means but lose their local and historical color, communication has not been achieved either. Translators should therefore know their readers, anticipate possible losses and try to compensate for them in other ways.

It remains for me to point out, in conclusion, that I have tried to describe and systematize actual occurrences, rather than to prescribe any rules that translators should feel obliged to follow. After all, the final decision is always theirs, and nobody else's.

Index

addressee, importance of role 29
adequacy 65–6, 70: defined 48, 51–2, 53, 55–6; demand for 52
Allen, F. *Only Yesterday* 27–8
allomorphous units 33–4
Andres, A., "Distance in time and translation" 12
Anokhin, P. 92
Antokol'skij *et al* 12
approximate translation 126
archaizing elements 11, 13, 15
articulation 94–5
asymmetry, paradigmatic 36; syntagmatic 35–6

background knowledge 103
Baetens Beardsmore, H. 61
Bally, Charles 35
Barkhudarov, L. 49–50, 66, 67
Bausch, Karl 69
Belyaev, B. 88, 94
Benediktov, B. 93–4
Big English–Russian Dictionary 22, 25, 28, 50
Byron, Lord, *Childe Harold* 54–5

calques 125; Bulgarian 59, 60–2
cataphoric reflection 92
Catford, J. 23–4, 65
channel capacity 105
cognitive approach 102–9
communication 80–1, 83, 88, 97–8; between author, translator and reader 14–15, 18

communicative situation 39
comparative linguistics 19
comprehension 76
conceptualization 94–6, 101
concreteness 49, 68; two levels 77–8
Constant, Benjamin, *Adolphe* 12
contextual meaning 20, 26–7
contextual theme (CT) 119, 120
contextual translation 126
convention 70, 74

derheme 119
desemantization 36, 38
difficulty 105–6

equivalence 34–5, 40, 42, 46, 65–6, 70–1, 74–5, 101, 102–3, 126; communicative 51, 52; defined 53; deviation from 52–4; establishment 49; full 51–2; historical context 47–8; of texts 50
equivalent correspondence 19–25
equivalent translation 11
European language league 59
experience 105
extralinguistic context 27–30

Fedorov, A. V. 68, 88, 98
Feurbach, Ludwig 112
film translation 6
Fitzgerald, F. Scott, *Tender is the Night* 30; *The Great Gatsby* 30

fixed correspondence 19–20
Foster, W. 29
free translation 46, 65, 66
functional sentence perspective (FSP) 120–1

Gachechiladze, G. R. 14
Gak, V. 27
Gal'perin, I. 22
genre and style 70, 71–2
geographical names 22, 119
Gorky, Maxim 1
grapheme 41, 42
Guardian, The 29
Gumpertz, J. J. 61

Hahn, Otto 118
Haugen, E. 61
Hegel, G. W. F. 82
Heidegger, M. 110
Hemingway, Ernest, *The Sun Also Rises* 53
Hieronymous 47
historical distance, four types 12–17

iconic mapping 106, 107
ideational product 111–15
identifier–classifier groups 118
identity 84–5
idioms 44
image-schematic mapping 106–7
implicit/explicit configurations 108–9
interlingual influence 58
invariance 50
ironic relativism 110
isomorphous units 33, 35, 38

Jakobsen, *Frau Maria Grube* 12

Kacnel'son, S. 24
Kalashnikova, E. 30
Kardosh, L. 13
Kashkin, I. 54–5
Komissarov, V. 40, 48, 72
Kurochkin, B. 67

Lakoff, G. and Johnson, M. 106

language 83; double existence 113–14; source/target 43, 95, 125–8; use 106–9
Lee, Harper, *To Kill a Mockingbird* 30, 49
Leont'iev, A. N. 89, 97
level of translation 45
Levik, V. 55
lexemes 38
lexico-grammatical units 34
Lilova, Anna 15
linguistic approach 9, 13, 14–15, 16, 20, 21–5; development 103–5; reality 68–9; units 49; usage 70, 72–4, 72–3
literal translation 45, 58, 61, 65, 66, 101
literary approach 13–14, 25–7
Ll'f, I. and Petrov, E., *The Twelve Chairs* (US: *Diamonds to Sit On*) 53
logico-semantic basis 19, 20, 21
L'vov, S. 12–13
Lyudskanov, A. 8

mapping, various 106–9
material thinking 82–3
metaphorical mapping 107
monorheme 119
Morozov, M. 55
morpheme 40–1, 42–3
My Fair Lady 52

neologisms 125–6
neutralization 36–7
Nida, E. A. 105
non-contextual theme (NCT) 119, 120
normative–evaluative system 78–9, 83–4, 85–6
norms 54, 58; analysis 63–4; codifying/imposing 3; components 69–75; establishment of principles 67–9; notion 64; problem 64
nostalgia 39

object–scheme code 93, 95, 96
objective situation 27–8
one-domain mapping 106, 107

Index 131

pedagogy 32
Pegacheva, Z. 88
philosophy 33
phoneme 41–2
phrasemes 57–62
phrasemic code switching 60
Phraseological Dictionary of the Bulgarian Language 60
phraseological units 44
polysemy 33
pragmatic: function 70, 74; setting 73, 74, 81
predicate-splitting mapping 106, 108
predicative unit (PU) 115–19
psychological aspects 3, 8, 88–99

Rabelais, *Gargantua and Pantagruel* 12
Random House Dictionary 102
realia 122–8; classified 123–5; ethnographic 123–4; geographic 124; importance 127; nature 127; and time 124–5
reality 120
réglementation 64, 68
Reiss, Katherina and Vermeer, Hans J. 9, 48, 50
Retsker, J. 49, 65
Revzin, I. and Rozentsveig, B. 66, 68, 88
rheme (R) 119
Rossel, V. 54
Rubinstein, S. 90

Salinger, J. D., *The Catcher in the Rye* 43, 49–50
Schveitser, A. 8
self-organizing system (SOS) 85–6
sense 110; defined 111; separation 115
sentences 43–5
Shakespeare, William, *Othello* 55
Shaw, George Bernard 28; *Pygmalion* 52–3
Shengeli, G. 54–5
shifts 24
Silverstone, Sidney 28
simultaneous interpretation 92, 96, 98

social knowledge 113
Solodukho, E. M. 61, 62
speech activity 28, 88–99; complex 97; defined 89–91; object 90
Square Peg, A 54
style 80–6

text, comparative analysis 119; inner pattern 82; interpretation 78–9; primary/secondary 51; religious 73–4; scientific 126; segments 117–19; source/target 52–3, 55, 58, 66, 72, 104–6, 109; as unified structure 80–1
time, importance 11
tradition, evolution 54
transformation 34–8, 40, 41
transformed form 112–13
transitions 24
translation, as activity 78; choice of level 66–7; complexity 92–4, 96; as continuous process 94; criticism 71; defined 77–80, 88, 91; degree of creativity 8–9; evaluation 75; functional 6–7; genetic 7; influence 60; inner/outer attributes 80; as meaningful act 2; micro/macro 24–5; as multilevel/multilateral 6; phenomenon of growing old 16; as product of history 5; reality 87; results 70; rules 68; secondary nature 98–9; specificity 98; structure and content 7–8; theories 19–21, 34, 64–5; three stages 94–6; tradition in 1–4; use of 63
translational transliteration 41
translator, requirements 58; task 19, 40, 69
transleme 40
transparent translation 11–12
transposition 36, 37–8
Twain, Mark 60
two-domain mapping 106

understanding, as correlation 80–2
unit of translation 39, 43; defined 40–1

variant correspondence 18, 20, 25–6
Vygotskij, L. 90

Wittgenstein, L. 110; *Tractatus* 48
Wodehouse, P. G. 60

words, combination 44; occasional/usual 26; redundancy 38

Zimnyaya, I. and Chernov, G. 92–3

For Product Safety Concerns and Information please contact our EU
representative GPSR@taylorandfrancis.com
Taylor & Francis Verlag GmbH, Kaufingerstraße 24, 80331 München, Germany

www.ingramcontent.com/pod-product-compliance
Lightning Source LLC
Chambersburg PA
CBHW052031300426
44116CB00024B/1850